Jackie Stewart's
Principles of
Performance Driving

Jackie Stewart's Principles of Performance Driving

Edited by Alan Henry

Hazleton Publishing, Richmond, Surrey

The editor would like to offer his acknowledgements and thanks to those who have helped in the preparation of this book: Harry Calton, Stuart Turner, Peter Ashcroft of the Ford Motor Company; Judy Chilcote of IMG; Mike Greasley, David Tremayne, Nigel Roebuck, Eoin Young, Maurice Hamilton. They put up with more than anyone would know in 1985!

PUBLISHER
Richard Poulter

EXECUTIVE PUBLISHER
Elizabeth Le Breton

PUBLISHING ASSISTANT
Jane Payton

HOUSE EDITOR
Stephen Spark

DESIGNER
Tony Baldwin

Colour Photography by:
Diana Burnett
Elf France
LAT Photographic
Nigel Snowdon

Black & White Photography by:
LAT Photographic
Goodyear Tire & Rubber Company
Ford Motor Company
Dougie Firth
Alan Henry
Sue Atkinson (Mike Roles Studios)
Jim Bamber
Camera Press London
Haymarket Picture Library
Trevor Jones (Allsport Photographic)

ISBN 0-905138-43-0

Typeset by C. Leggett & Son Ltd, Mitcham, Surrey.

Printed in the Netherlands by drukkerij de lange/van Leer bv, Deventer.

UK distribution by Osprey Publishing Limited, 12-14 Long Acre, London WC2E 9LP.

North American distribution by Motorbooks International, Osceola, Wisconsin 54020, USA.

Contents

Foreword

It has often been said that, next to casting doubts upon his virility, the worst insult you could offer to any man is to criticise his driving. Yet the accident statistics make it all too horrifyingly clear that there is, and I suspect always will be, vast scope for improvement in driving standards.

The connection between competition driving and road safety may at first appear to be a tenuous one, but as Jackie Stewart explains in this fascinating book, far from there being any conflict between the two, the principles that make for successful driving on the race track are equally applicable on the road. And a driver who takes the trouble to improve his skill, it is argued, is likely also to be a much safer driver.

There can be no-one better qualified than triple World Champion Jackie Stewart to teach the finer points of car control and roadcraft which he put into practice so successfully in his racing days. I can say this with confidence since a few years ago I was lucky enough to have a lengthy driving session with Jackie at Silverstone, when I was able to experience at first hand the extraordinary delicacy and finesse with which he handles a car. I have never forgotten that lesson and I have no doubt that the Stewart principles, even when inexpertly applied as in my own case, can help make a much better and smoother driver.

This book, which contains the distilled wisdom of one of the most talented drivers ever to take the wheel, is the next best thing to being in a car with Jackie Stewart himself. I cannot believe that anyone who takes the least interest in improving his driving skill, whether novice or veteran, would not find it of absorbing interest and, dare I say it, of considerable benefit to his or her own technique.

H.R.H. The Duke of Kent
President
The Automobile Association

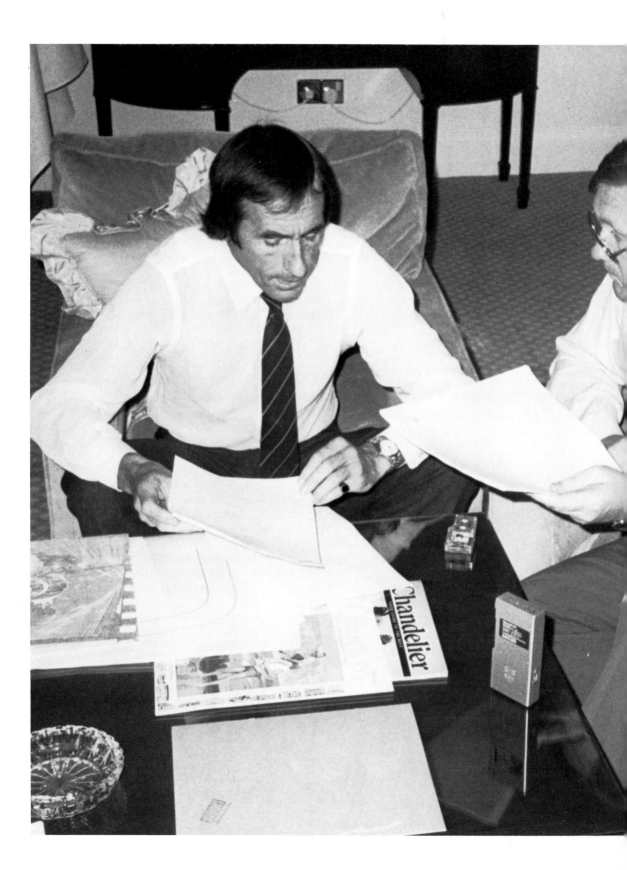

Introduction

When I finished writing *Faster* with Peter Manso, I swore I would never write another book. I'm not a person who finds it easy to write, because of the dyslexia and learning disabilities I suffered in my youth. The frustrations of taping sessions and proof readings made me so fed up that, when the book finally came out, I never read it as a finished item.

I'm not a person who feels comfortable producing the written word. I therefore have to tape everything; the spoken word often becomes subtly and inadvertently changed when transferred to paper. It has therefore been my pleasure to work with Alan Henry on this book because I have found, as in my past, my train of thought is often invigorated by a question, a conversation, or a point made by another person which has allowed me to amplify a particular specific aspect or detail.

I always felt that this learning disability helped me in later life because I was so frustrated as a youngster experiencing difficulty in assimilating the necessary information at school because I was never certain things were being explained to me in sufficient detail. Dealing with these problems made me very much more determined than I might otherwise have been.

If there are passages in this book where I deal with matters a second time, perhaps with slightly different emphasis, it is because they need to be reiterated to ensure that the particular point is driven home. Some people with learning problems and dyslexia have been great orators – Sir Winston Churchill and Einstein to name but two – and one part of my moderate success in life has been that I've been able to communicate well with other people.

I hope this book helps to communicate what I feel about driving motor cars, whether it be on road or track, to a wider audience and to allow them to understand what I strove for in terms of the technique I was able to develop. I wasn't aiming primarily to be the best Grand Prix driver, but to be better than *me*. In the end, what I was doing was striving against myself rather than against the competition. The competition all made mistakes but I alone was privy to my own errors of judgement. Many were never noticed by outside observers, but I knew they had happened and was always frustrated by my own weakness in having allowed them to occur.

Hopefully, this book will assist readers to become more self-conscious about the art of driving and to be able to apply the Stewart Principles to their performance, whether on the road or in a competitive circuit environment.

Chapter 1
The Basic Qualities

There's no doubt in my mind that any particular talented individual in the world who excels in any specific area, whether it be in sport, industry, politics or religion, has been given a gift from God. This applies to any walk of life. There are a great many people given those gifts. I always relate it to motor racing because that is one area in which I'm most able to judge the competence and application of those who reach the highest level.

This is true also for other occupations. Take, for example, the airline pilot who walks around the airport with that air of superiority, with the gold bands around his arm and the braid on his hat; or the rather supercilious surgeon who strides through the hospital wards with an air of authority and esteem because he's saving people's lives, and therefore his presence radiates self-confidence and encourages people to look up to him.

The reality is that, like racing drivers, there are hundreds of thousands of doctors and airline pilots, though perhaps only thirty can claim to be the very best at any one time. In my opinion, out of those thirty drivers only about six have been exceptionally talented. Out of those six I have never known more than three who were extraordinary. And out of those three there might be one or two geniuses.

If you bear this in mind in relation to those doctors who stride, or those pilots who pose, you suddenly realise how absurd the whole system is as to how good we all think we are. How many planes have we been in that have not greased themselves onto the runway? How many times has a plane arrived at the terminal building and suddenly dipped its nose, causing everybody who has stood up prematurely to stagger forward? It hasn't been a smooth, gentle roll to a halt. How many doctors have made ugly incisions which cannot be repaired, even with plastic surgery? How many forgotten to take out swabs, or have performed operations which are not the work of a real artist?

Each person, whether an accountant, engineer, electrician, lawyer, poltician, military or religious leader, is bracketed within the same limits of proficiency. I suggest that in this book we examine the sheer unadulterated talent that God has given us. God gave to that surgeon and that airline pilot a gift, but it was how he or she has manicured, manipulated and extended that inborn talent, through their own resources, desire and commitment, that has brought them to the level of those immensely successful thirty Grand Prix drivers . . . or those six extraordinarily talented individuals, or those last one or two geniuses. They were all given the gift and, in most cases, they did not get more than others. It was how they applied themselves to developing that gift that made the difference.

Juan Manuel Fangio is seen here in a streamlined Mercedes-Benz at Monza in 1954. He won five World Championship titles before retiring in 1958 at the age of 47. A cool, calculating and extremely shrewd driver, the great Argentinian was a fine tactician, the classic embodiment of a 'thinking driver'. He was at his peak during an era which is often romanticised by current observers, but his achievements did not come about by accident. His success showed that he must have worked out his strategy and his approach to the profession with meticulous precision.

In this book we hope to be able to describe to the reader the best ways of recognising those weaknesses, pitfalls and errors that can prevent a person stepping up to the next stage of understanding and becoming a better driver, whether in competition or in ordinary road driving. If we recognise that there is this enormous range of talent to start with, we have to recognise that there is much to be learned. I don't expect to be able to answer all the questions because I certainly don't know all the answers.

From my earliest years of driving I had a hungry enthusiasm to be able to control the car, to be able to feel what it was like at the limits of adhesion. It was when I was very young on a wintry day when the snow was packed in front of our family garage – R.P. Stewart and Sons in Dumbuck, near Dumbarton, Scotland – that I took an old Austin 16 out at no more than 10 mph and caused the back end to slide because I applied too much power. The thrill I got from feeling that car slide and then being able to apply what I

know today was opposite lock, and feel that car being controlled . . . well, I just couldn't wait for winter!

Those very early days driving round my father's garage were great. I was about nine years of age in that elderly dark blue Austin and had to sit on a two gallon can to be able to see out beneath the top of the heavy bakelite steering wheel and over the top of the dashboard. I revelled in possessing the intuition which allowed me to control my slides. Later I was given a chance to drive up Milton Hill behind our garage. I used to go up with Hugh Burch and Willie White, two mechanics who worked in the garage. I talked them into letting me drive, although this was of course totally illegal. I was 12 years old by now and this enabled me to have some practice changing gear, get up to 30 mph, go round corners and change direction. This gave me a little insight as to what I wanted to do.

By that stage my brother Jimmy Stewart – Jim, as he was always known in our family – was driving fast cars. He is eight years older, so by the time I was nine or ten, Jim was already starting. He was racing an MG TC, then later a Healey Silverstone. He was a very clean driver, very smooth; a very good driver. In those sprints, hill climbs and races he used to compete against people like John Melvin in his Frazer-Nash Le Mans Replica, a fantastic car which cost £3500 in those days, Jimmy Gibbon in his special, Jack Walton in his Frazer-Nash, John Brown in his HWM and Hartley-Whyte in his Jaguar. Wonderful cars . . .

Jim later drove for Ecurie Ecosse, Aston Martin and the Jaguar factory teams, so I was given the bug of racing by my brother on the way to these events, crouching behind the aero screens in his MG or the Healey, wearing my flying helmet. And I think that even then I began to appreciate the difference between a good driver and a bad driver.

It's similar to handling a shot gun. You handle it easily, but with respect. The way in which you address the gun to your body indicates whether you are a natural or not, in just the same way as somebody holds the steering wheel of a car. There is even some suggestion that a woman can spot a good lover by the way he handles his car, the steering wheel and his gearchange. A car is not a vehicle which accepts abrasive, heavy-handed methods. A performance vehicle is a very sensitive and subtle piece of engineering. Direct it in a gentle and progressive fashion and you'll get much better performance out of it than from a car that is manhandled and abused. You can recognise somebody who has some sensitivity, and that, most often, is a natural gift.

However, this physical aptitude is not always matched to the same degree by mental faculties. I have met many great natural drivers who, in some way or another, have let themselves down by their inability, mentally, to utilise that talent in an appropriate fashion.

One of the greatest natural talents I ever saw drive a racing car was Gilles Villeneuve. His flair for extraordinary car control under the most acute angles of slide, for example, could only have been inbred. It was certainly no mechanical movement.

It was intuitive, yet he never achieved greatness because his mental attitude within the car was not synchronised with the physical attributes which allowed him to control those vehicles.

You saw Gilles Villeneuve over-driving more often than you saw him under-driving. Had he gone slower, he would have gone faster. How many times was he seen trying to drive away in a car so hopelessly damaged that it had no chance at all of continuing the race? But his head had jumped out of gear. You cannot have your heart ruling your head. You must always be able to control all your elements, your emotions and your logic. Perhaps Gilles was never able to tell when it was right to drive at the absolute limit. Because if you drive to the limit with a badly adjusted chassis, the wrong tyres for that temperature or that track surface, or if the engine has lost some of its edge, what do you do? You have to acknowledge it. It's no use driving a dog so hard that it dies. You need that dog to take you across the ice pack. So you have to stroke that dog, allow it some air, let it breathe. You've got to give that car some space to accommodate its inadequacies.

Of course, this notion doesn't always find favour with the critics. My view of many critics, though, is very simple. Most of them have never really done it: they are talkers and observers. If you are going to drive a motor car to the limit of its capabilities, I'm not suggesting that you only do it when you are running in first or second position. But do it with your head. It can and should happen any time.

Jim Clark was a man of contrasts and had a huge influence on me during my early racing years. I do not believe that Jimmy ever considered how or why he produced competitive Formula 1 performances – he just had such intuitive brilliance that he never needed to worry about it. I finished second behind him in three Grands Prix during 1965 and felt very satisfied indeed when I beat his record of 25 Grand Prix career victories during my final season, 1973.

When I went into the pits on the seventh lap at Monza in 1973 with a flat tyre after picking up a nail, I started off again last by quite a margin. But I drove as good a race, technically, as I had ever driven in my career. Not because I thought 'let's have a thrash', but because I felt obliged to catch up. I had a reason, because to finish fourth in that race would win me the World Championship.

Now, I have to tell you that when I left the pits that day I had no hope in my mind of getting up to fourth. But I knew I had to drive as well as I could. I drove the car to the limit of my ability and the car's ability and I was rewarded by coming through the field to finish fourth. I had something to aim for. I wasn't burning myself or the car out for no good reason.

I noticed the crowd getting excited. They were looking at me in a way that they weren't looking at me when I left the pits. They wanted to see me do well, so the spirit of the whole occasion was getting to them and to me. To start with I was getting signals from Ken Tyrrell saying '−14s ASCARI or FANGIO' to keep me amused, to stop me becoming bored and despondent. Soon I found myself catching somebody significant, somebody I needed to pass, so on that particular day I was doing something extra.

Now, on a day such as that, the Villeneuve syndrome could have worked

19

Above: *very much a driver after my own style, Niki Lauda consciously and consistently worked at removing all the emotion from his driving technique throughout his highly successful career. Calculating, patient and easy on the machinery, Lauda approached his motor racing in a detached, clinical manner and reaped the reward by taking three World Championship titles.*

Above right: *Ivan Lendl in dramatic tennis action, an example of a highly professional sportsman from another sphere. However demanding and competitive sports of this nature may be, at the end of the day they are unlikely to exact a physical toll much beyond pulled muscles or possibly a sprained wrist. A mistake in tennis does not have the dramatic and potentially dangerous consequences of an error behind the wheel of a competition car.*

totally. But while doing it, I still wasn't sliding the car, making it look more spectacular because, had I done that, I would have lost time, and would have put up the tyre temperatures to the point where they would have gone off, lost performance and grip.

What I had to do was to drive with my head. You must take stock mentally of what you are doing. Now, some purists applauded Jackie Stewart on that day, but had they known how clinically I was going about the exercise, they might not have been so pleased.

Personally, I think I did the sport more justice by being successful than simply having driven in an uninhibited, unrestrained and spectacular manner. When we think of the purists, we tend to think of some of the great names from the past. But I would dare to suggest that if they were here today to speak for themselves, they would admit that they didn't do much without some thought: they were too successful, too good to depend on great flair alone.

One of the masters of that approach was Fangio. When he drove perhaps his greatest race round the Nürburgring in 1957 to catch Hawthorn and Collins, he was driving out of his skin and didn't fly off the road. He drove a uniquely spirited, fantastically exciting race. But that was because he was such a great driver, and such drives occasionally emerged from Fangio, like I'm sure they've emerged in the name of Jim Clark, or in the name of Stirling Moss. Or, hopefully, in the name of Jackie Stewart. For me, maybe, it was Nürburgring '68 in the wet or Monza '73 in the dry.

Therefore I think it is important to remember that, when you recall these great drives, by great drivers whose names are down in the record book, such as Caracciola, or Nuvolari, then Ascari, Farina, Fangio, Clark and Lauda, they were all very calculating drivers. They knew that the gift was there, that it had to be manipulated and directed towards the most important areas.

Motor Sport's Denis Jenkinson often criticised me for being clinical. That was one of the best compliments he ever paid me, although it had not been intended as such. I really feel that to be one of the very few, you have to remove a great many elements that are, I suppose, ingredients that people like to see. Unfortunately, those are the very elements which can be your downfall.

Take Jochen Rindt, for example. Denis Jenkinson was not convinced that Jochen was the great talent I believed him to be, and declared he would shave off his beard if Jochen ever won a Grand Prix – which he did of course, and Denis lost his beard. Jochen in his early days displayed that flamboyant, natural God-given style of motor racing bravado: he could get a car sideways and bring it back from almost any attitude.

In his Formula 2 days, that was easy to do because the cars allowed it; they were light and not overpowered. As he matured, and as he was an intelligent person, he recognised that those things did not go together with success. In the second half of his 1969 season, and certainly in his 1970 season, he was a changed man.

By the British Grand Prix in 1969 he was wonderful to race with. He was no longer the Jochen Rindt of Pau in an F2 car whom I had followed in fear and trepidation because I thought 'any minute now I'll be running over pieces of debris'. No, at Silverstone, he was the epitome of smoothness and elegance behind the wheel and as good a driver as I have ever raced against. He and I were both very much on form that day. We both drove cars which handled well and it was one of the best races of my life, as far as memories are concerned.

But it was never allowed to reach a conclusion. The end plate of his rear wing came undone and began rubbing against his tyre. Jochen and I were very good friends so I was a little confused as to how to play it. We could obviously communicate to a very limited extent and I was left with the dilemma of deciding whether to tell him about something which could potentially have been dangerous. But would he think that Jackie was either trying to fool him, or take advantage, or what?

In the end I did pull alongside on Hangar Straight and point at his problem in hope that he would be able to see it in his rear-view mirror and make his own judgement. Jochen did in fact stop to have the end plate ripped off, resuming about 30 seconds or so behind me, in a strong second place. He later made a second stop for fuel which dropped him to fourth.

That was a hell of a race, but it was with a driver who had matured. And there was a driver who had extraordinary natural talent, but who was able to recognise that its unadulterated use was an unsuccessful method of driving. What he had to do was harness that enormous natural gift by mental aptitude. That's where I separate Jochen and Gilles. Ronnie Peterson was another example; he never harnessed it totally. He harnessed it better than Gilles, but not as well as Jochen.

Another example from the Sixties and Seventies, Chris Amon, had a great natural skill but was not able to marshal his mental attitude sufficiently to make use of it. In his case, he failed to make sound business decisions regarding who he drove for, the mechanics he worked with or the motivation of his team.

Considering some drivers of the present, let's look at Keke Rosberg. Keke, for me, has developed: and he has developed partly, at least, thanks to the increase of power offered in recent years by the arrival of the turbo charged era in Formula 1. The incredibly high tyre temperatures which result from this extra power demand extra sensitivity by the driver towards his tyres.

I don't think Keke has yet totally overcome his basic pleasurable exuberance but, in a way, he has come of age. He has graduated. His drive, for example, at Paul Ricard in 1985 was excellent: he was fully aware that he couldn't overdo things with his tyres and yet he drove with superb balance to take what in years gone past would never have been a second place.

He knows what he has to do but he is still a little over-aggressive; he still has trouble restraining his exuberance, his flair, his tendency to drive around problems rather than eliminating them. I think the future may show us a more sophisticated Keke Rosberg, particularly since joining McLaren. That will make him increasingly useful to the designers he works with. I think some of those designers have not been over-enthusiastic about the amount of information they received from him in the past.

So although Keke has taken, perhaps, rather longer than he might have liked to mature, I think he is now maturing.

René Arnoux has always been a driver that I have thought of in the same mould as Keke; a similar type to Gilles Villeneuve. A hell-raiser of a competitor who drives the only way he knows, by the seat of his pants and to the best of his abilities. There's no half speed for René Arnoux. He's a highly nervous individual, over-tense and over-wound. You only need to look at his eyes; they dart, the pupils always seem to be enlarged.

He drives a car in the same fashion. A Formula 1 car is basically nervous and highly strung, it darts and dives too aggressively, so the driver who is more nervous than the car makes the situation even worse. There is no flowing, mellow, controlled style. His is an abrupt turn-in, abrupt application of throttle and brakes. There isn't that liquidity about the whole performance. It is for these reasons that I never thought René Arnoux would ever reach the dizzy heights of greatness. I thought he would be very fast, a great pole-position merchant – which he has been during his career – but I never felt he would be a consistent winner.

It is difficult for me to assess how well he will be able to pick up the strands of his career since leaving Ferrari after the first race of 1985. It has to be said that Ferrari was a fantastic team for him, although whether he can thrive in another environment remains to be seen. It is a measure of the uncompromising nature of the business that only a couple of months after Arnoux had withdrawn from Formula 1, it was as if he had never existed. Nobody was even discussing him. The waves close over you very quickly in Grand Prix racing – and the people within the sport are very fickle. I can think of drivers who have attracted great adulation and respect who suddenly fell from prominence through lack of success, and are suddenly ignored by the same people who were cheering them shortly before. It has happened to me, I can tell you.

As much as René Arnoux is over-nervous, Ayrton Senna is mellow. As much as Keke goes on and off the throttle with abruptness, so Senna does it calmly, smoothly, almost slowly. I have to say that he is my kind of driver. If somebody else was writing this book, his talent, skill and success might be regarded in a different way, but, for me, the way that he drives is *the* way to race and to drive.

When you drive in those slow, fluid, controlled movements, you have so much more time in hand to do things. When you're doing them in paper-hanger-in-a-thunderstorm fashion, there is no time to concentrate on the subtleties of your driving. You are either coming off a problem or going into another.

If you are on the throttle, with anything between 500 and 1000 bhp

Trap shooting was my first sport. The pleasure, satisfaction and sense of achievement involved in handling a gun correctly and efficiently provided me with another competitive environment before I ever raced. I am convinced that it helped me deal with the inevitable disappointments involved in any competitive activity and gave me something of a head start in this respect when I really became serious about my motor racing.

working against you, any excess movement exaggerates the period in which you are handling that particular problem. All those elongated experiences take up time, so you're left with little or no creativity. It's the same as if you're very busy in life: so busy answering the phone, so busy trying to reach a meeting you are already late for, so busy getting to the bank before it closes or preparing a report at the last moment . . . you're not allowed any thinking time, distilling time. You have no time to think about putting together a better performance; all you are doing is keeping up, you are a passenger instead of being a pacesetter.

Ayrton Senna is a pacesetter. He sets the pace of his car to that track, to that speed. The Master of Going Faster, as George Harrison put it! If you are just a passenger, it's like riding a big dipper. The G-forces don't allow you to reposition yourself, to make yourself more comfortable. It's all too much!

Senna's mechanics tell you that he uses fewer brake pads – just as I did when I was paired with Graham Hill at BRM back in the Sixties. Like Senna, though, I was prompted by no conscious thought to drive in a particular way to conserve the machinery. That's just the way I drove – and Senna did that *vis-à-vis* Elio de Angelis at Lotus throughout 1985.

Another example of Senna's class could be seen at Monaco. It is a very busy circuit on which it is extremely difficult to make the car seem manageable and, somehow, look slow. I was out on the track when he did his quick time – and it was very noticeable to the expert eye.

I don't expect Ayrton Senna to reach his full potential for at least two full years after the end of the 1985 season. In fact, in those two years he will encounter occasions when the brilliance with which he has been credited by many will be called into question. His performance in the 1985 Australian Grand Prix, for example, was an eye-opener. He certainly did not seem to have his mind in gear: he did things which you would expect from a bright-eyed, bushy-tailed young driver who had no control over his emotions. It was not a pretty sight, but at least Senna proved that we're all fallible and nobody is perfect. I would expect it to have been a very good lesson for him.

However, Rome wasn't built in a day and you don't become Einstein overnight at the age of 25. It takes experience, consistent performance and racing miles to hone and manicure the basic talent which he undoubtedly possesses.

It is a definite fact that some highly promising drivers look simply like shooting stars, apparently peaking early and then experiencing a dropping-off of form before coming back to confirm their reputation in a more solid fashion. It happened to Mario Andretti and it happened to me: I finished third in the World Championship in my first Formula 1 season and won two races, one of them a Championship Grand Prix. That was 1965, but I then experienced what many observers deemed highly disappointing seasons in 1966 and 1967 before coming on strong again and reassert myself in 1968.

Both Tony Brise and Tom Pryce were examples of this in 1975, although they were killed before they could have their 'second wind', but the promise was already taking longer than anticipated to mature. You come in with this youthful exuberance, driving by the seat of your pants, and it seems the easiest thing to do at the time, harnessing all that inherent talent. But you cannot maintain that flow of adrenalin through the system to keep up that kind of performance, which is really in excess of what you should be giving on a regular basis. You have to come down and find a plateau at a lower

With a rear tyre disintegrating as it pulls off its rim, Gilles Villeneuve none the less presses on in dauntless stye during the 1979 Dutch Grand Prix at Zandvoort. Gilles had an extraordinary inbred flair for outstanding car control but his whole mental attitude caused him to over-drive too often during his career. If he had tried a little less he might have achieved a great deal more.

level, then slowly and very progressively get back up by learning how to cut corners, where to conserve your energy, and understanding where potential mistakes can be made. You can appear well-adjusted after coming in from a few hot laps, but you know that's not the case. You know you've just come in from one hell of a drive. You can't keep on putting in Oscar-winning performances in every picture! There isn't a movie star who does it and there isn't an athlete who does it. It is almost impossible to do and if you're driving a racing car that's an even more complicated issue because of all the mechanical aspects to consider.

It is necessary to identify this problem, however. Funnily enough, although Ayrton Senna demonstrated his considerable skill in 1985, he could have a relatively uncompetitive season to follow. If he had wanted to move teams, in my opinion, 1986 would have been a year to choose because then his 'off year' could have been put down partly to his change of environment.

For me, the enigma of being a successful Grand Prix driver is the necessity of being such an amalgam of talents. You must be able, in the end, to bring forth many exceptional abilities. There are so many different elements involved in producing the kind of success we all look for beyond just steering the car.

The best opportunities must be recognised, and that leads you into the field of business decisions. Who should you drive for, who is the chief

One of my most personally rewarding races was the 1973 Italian Grand Prix at Monza where I finished fourth and clinched the World Championship title for the third time in my career. Early in the race I had to make a pit stop to change a deflated rear tyre, then climbed back through the field from last place after a really satisfying performance. It was an example of controlled effort and energy, though, and I like to think that on this particular day my drive was something a little special.

27

designer, who is the chief mechanic? Which offers should be accepted and which quietly refused? And then, once you've made a choice and taken into account all the ingredients available to you, how can you motivate people into being even better than they ever dreamed they could be? By your enthusiasm, by your dedication, by courting their talent and getting them to do things for you, you can help people discover new areas of knowledge within themselves.

I don't think that Roger Hill (Chief Mechanic for Tyrrell Racing to this day, who brought me to three World Championships) when still in New Zealand ever thought he would rise to becoming one of the finest motor racing engineers. But he came over to Britain and he stayed. He has been given a gift of talent just as his drivers have and he has manipulated that gift to a higher level than just accepting it and saying 'Thank you very much' – because that's what a lot of people do. He became an extraordinary mechanic.

I was able, luckily (and I say luckily because we can talk about luck later), to see real talent and potential in some of the people I became associated with. Chris Amon was, in my opinion, in as good a position as anyone to choose where to go and when to go, but somehow he made the wrong choices. The first good decision that I made was going to BRM in 1965. I was being courted heavily by Colin Chapman and it was a very intoxicating thought to go and join Jim Clark, another Scot, whom I admired enormously and with whom I'd shared an apartment in Mayfair. I was very much in awe of his talent, but it wouldn't have worked for me and I was certainly aware of that.

I could have gone to Cooper, but I chose BRM because it was a good team and I knew that I needed a team that wouldn't push me too hard too soon. They had Graham Hill as their number one driver and anybody who came along as number two was going to be just that. Nevertheless, I saw in Graham a talent not as great as Jim Clark's, in sheer driving skill, but also an enormous determination and a wealth of knowledge and information I could learn from. And, funnily enough, I didn't think there was much I could learn from Jimmy, because his natural talent was so great that sometimes I don't think he knew how he did it. Had he thought a lot about it – and I think, towards the end, he was becoming able to see for himself how to channel this talent most positively – I would have been able to learn a great deal more.

To some extent I don't think Colin Chapman allowed him to think about it. Colin was such an incredibly influential man in Jim Clark's life, such an integral part of his success, that what Colin said Jimmy did. And I think that it was only late in his career that he was seeing some holes, if you like, in what Colin Chapman might have been saying, and he himself was getting ready to make some quite big decisions about how he wanted things done. But he was carried along on Colin's magic carpet for a long time, and very successfully too. I think I made a pretty good decision in going to BRM at the start of my career – and they were wonderful to me.

I also made the right choice by going to Ken Tyrrell and not to Ferrari in 1968. I nearly went to Ferrari. These decisions all form part of an overall package and they must be considered.

One of the unique things about the business of motor racing that makes it different from football, basketball, rugby or baseball, is that in these team sports other people mainly make decisions for you. You are just part of a policy decision and you go along with it. Pele was an extraordinary soccer player talent, but his manager made the decisions. Pele got into the bus or

Fangio really pressing on in a dramatically oversteering slide during the 1957 French Grand Prix at Rouen at the wheel of his Maserati 250F. On several occasions during his career the Argentinian suddenly produced a blistering performance out of the bag, exemplifying the way top drivers can rise above themselves and produce that little bit extra. This is what sets them apart. His drive at the Nürburgring the same season (right), when he shattered the lap record repeatedly on his way to victory, falls into the same category.

As Jochen Rindt matured, so he became an ever more formidable adversary. He was a supremely intelligent individual and quickly realised that an extrovert, opposite-lock driving style did not necessarily go hand-in-hand with success. By the time this picture was taken of his Lotus 49B leading my Matra MS80 during the 1969 British GP at Silverstone, Jochen was a changed man. He did not appear wild or aggressive in any way; in fact, he was the epitome of elegance and control. This battle with Austria's most loved driver was one of the most satisfying races of my career.

30

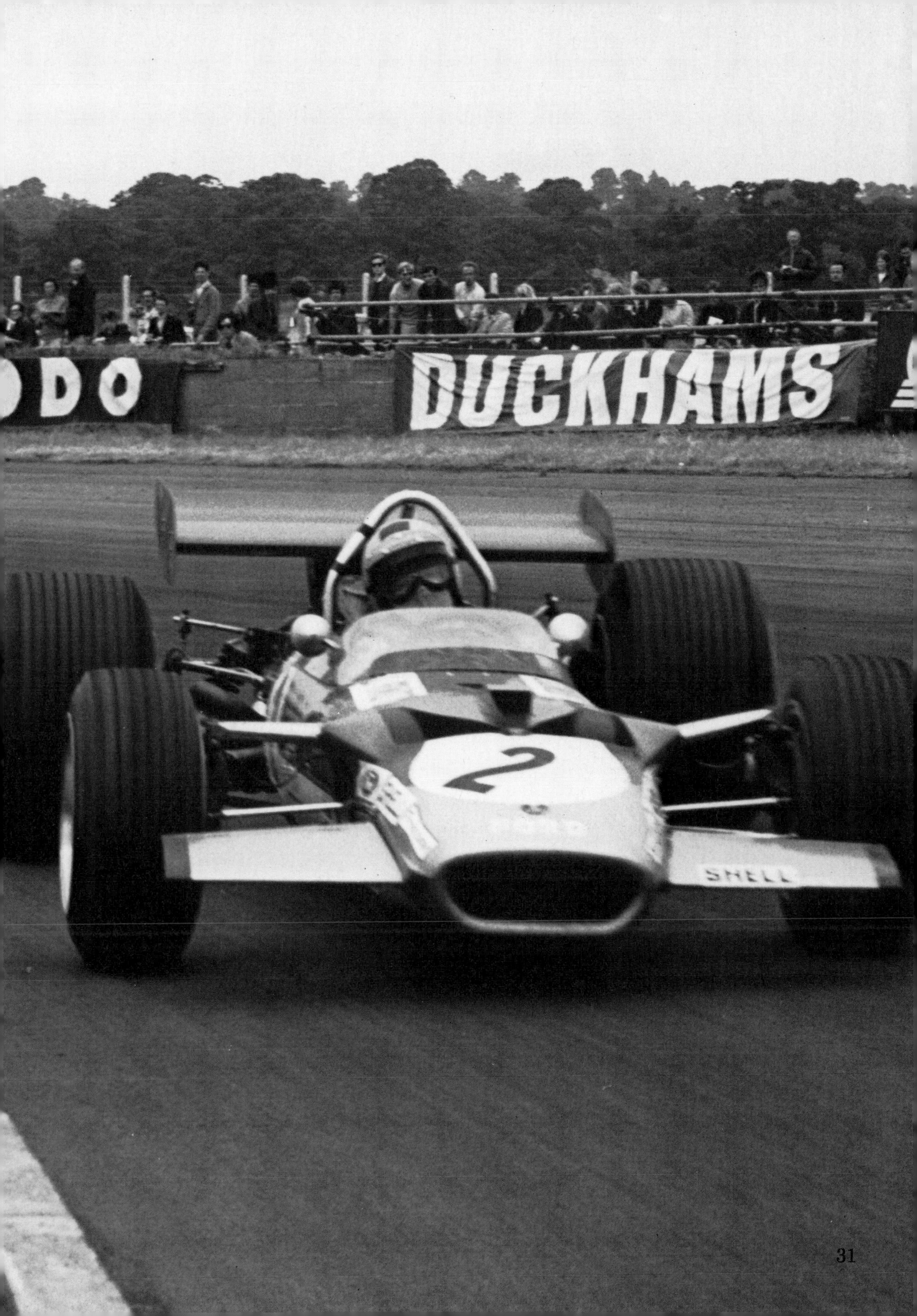
DUCKHAMS
SHELL

the train or the aircraft when he was told to. At the end of the day, all the travel arrangements were made by his team, all the major decisions of his professional life were made by others.

A racing driver is not like that. A competitive racing driver is much more a combination of talents. He makes his own travel arrangements. He does many things in life that most professional sportsmen are protected from. And he learns about life in a much broader spectrum, in my opinion. In athletics, for example, they have trainers who rule them. Zola Budd's trainer is paramount in what Zola Budd does. Sebastian Coe's father controls what he does. An athlete is dependent on that trainer, because he can take him to the peak – and the trainer can see from the outside, better than the athlete can from the inside, where that peak should be. That's not true in driving.

So the competitor has to be a more complete individual and that's why the mental attitude, in my opinion, overrides the natural gift. Assuming that God has given you that gift, the mental attitude to hone it, manicure it and shape it is going to make the difference between being a good, middle-of-the-road driver, and somebody quite special. And that applies whether you drive on the road or on the track, whether you play golf or tennis, or participate in any sport or activity. If, for example, you are going to let emotions interrupt logic or commonsense you are going to be less successful on the race track when you suddenly get angry with another competitor's action. Let's say he chops you off, let's say he's unashamedly rude in the ethics of driving. What are you going to do? Are you going to get mad or are you going to beat him? If you get mad you become irrational. You start saying 'I'm going to outbrake him. Whatever he does, I'm going to outbrake him'. And he does it, you interlock wheels, fly in the air and you both run off the road. Now is that good?

Or, do you say 'Right, now I'm going to apply myself. I'm going to see

Chris Amon was a highly popular driver endowed with tremendous natural talent, but he was never sufficiently organised to take best advantage of his own ability. He was always signing for the wrong team at the wrong time, a fact which highlights the necessity for a driver to be able to make correct calculations and decisions off the track as well as on.

I have always felt that Keke Rosberg might go even quicker if he abandoned his opposite-lock, deliberately oversteering style and concentrated on driving as smoothly and tidily as possible. Recently, since he got a very powerful turbocharged engine behind him in Formula 1, I get the impression that Keke is moderating that extrovert style quite considerably. This should allow him to realise even more of his natural flair.

where he's going wrong and I'm going to drive him into a mistake. I'm going to keep the heat on him, find where I can take advantage of him and then I'm going to snooker him.' The first time I can recall encountering this sort of situation in an F1 car was at the Silverstone International Trophy meeting in 1965, which I won from John Surtees' Ferrari. I remember that I'd driven a few races and I already knew which drivers I had to pay attention to. Close to the end of the race I came up to lap Lorenzo Bandini, who was driving the other Ferrari. I remember thinking 'My God, his pit will tell him that I'm leading the race and Surtees is second and he's going to hold me up.' By that time I had a little breathing space; not much, but a little. I thought that if he held me up I would lose the race. I could see it all happening. I remember seeing him, catching him, catching him . . . and then 'My God, I'm going to catch him at Becketts'. I was driving, convinced that he was going to retaliate, although it might never have been in his mind. But I recall driving into Becketts to make sure that, whatever he did, he couldn't cut in on me. I had over-driven him in, putting him in such a position on the race track that he couldn't retaliate. Now, I'm not saying that won me the race. But I know what didn't lose me the race – which is more important.

That's where this sort of awareness has to be very acute. It also happened in South Africa racing in a saloon event at Kyalami where Paul Hawkins had a Willment Galaxie and I was driving in place of Jim Clark in a Ford Lotus Cortina. I was sent to the Rand GP in a brand new Lotus 33 F1 car to drive not only in the F1 race, but also the Lotus Cortina in the supporting event. I could brake much later going into Crowthorne, so I would go down the inside into the corner. I would lean the Cortina against the Galaxie, and on occasions, go round the inside on two wheels. That was just part of the car's peculiar behaviour pattern. The front inside wheel would raise itself up a couple of feet off the ground, and then it would lift the rear wheel and it would be on two wheels. Paul was a great guy and he knew what was going on; he could always pass me on the straight, so I would lean on him to stop the car turning over!

Now, the man to beat out there was Basil van Rooyen. Basil was a very talented driver in my opinion, but I remember him telling me how his car was quicker than the factory cars, how they'd stripped the cars down and knew they were better than my works Lotus Cortina. Obviously the crowds were disappointed that Jim Clark didn't come out to drive the factory entry because they were waiting to see Basil put it over him; all they had to look at was this unknown boy Stewart. But Basil never really featured in the race. There had been enormous pressure on me, but I managed to beat this 'horrifically fast' local Lotus Cortina. I thought Basil had a huge natural talent, but he didn't allow it to be channelled mentally in the right direction because he was over-convinced about his car's ability. My experience is that anybody who has ever been any good at anything does not consider themselves to be better than anybody else.

How can anybody start strutting around saying that they are the best? I mean, what a wonderful platform to be knocked off. It's silly. Why put yourself in a position where, if you are beaten, you have to start making excuses? Why not acknowledge the fact that somebody else might be faster on a particular day? I know of several out-of-work racing drivers today who are entirely under the misapprehension that they were great and never given the right chance. Somehow or other racing dealt them an unfair blow. They remain convinced that they could have been the best.

As for those drivers who think they are so extraordinary – I have never

René Arnoux always struck me as having very nervous eyes which were always darting round the place, rather like his driving style, perhaps. He gives the impression of being tense and over-wound, not as relaxed as he should be to produce a fluid, measured performance behind the wheel. His much-publicised move from Renault to Ferrari produced several Grand Prix wins but René has never quite scaled the heights suggested by his early career achievements.

seen one of them make it. And if they haven't made it, that factor has probably been the reason for their failure – it may not have had anything to do with their natural talent. That cup might have been brimming over, but this mental attitude, this dogmatic over-confidence has probably not helped them.

I'm always fearful when I hear people say 'you've got to believe in yourself, you've got to believe you're the best, in order to win'. I think for me it's quite the reverse. When you believe you're the best you then take liberties with the opposition, you're always underestimating them, because you don't believe they're as good as you. When I go to a test track and drive a car, I never want to tell a test driver/engineer that I'm going to be better or faster than him because I've won three World Championships and 27 Grands Prix. It's crazy! This guy could be the one who's going to win 35 Grands Prix! So what sort of a fool am I putting myself up for? There's no point to it. It has no benefit at all for you to be under any false impression of your own talent. You can kid a lot of people, but you can't kid yourself. People turn round and say 'Jackie, you've been successful'. And that's true, up to a point. But am I as successful as I could have been? I'm really not sure. I think I could have done a lot better.

I appreciate what my shortcomings are. Perhaps I made some poor decisions – and I don't mean just about driving, I mean in general. I'm sitting here in very comfortable circumstances, but it doesn't prove that I've done everything right.

The other thing is that you must never, ever, go beyond the limits of your

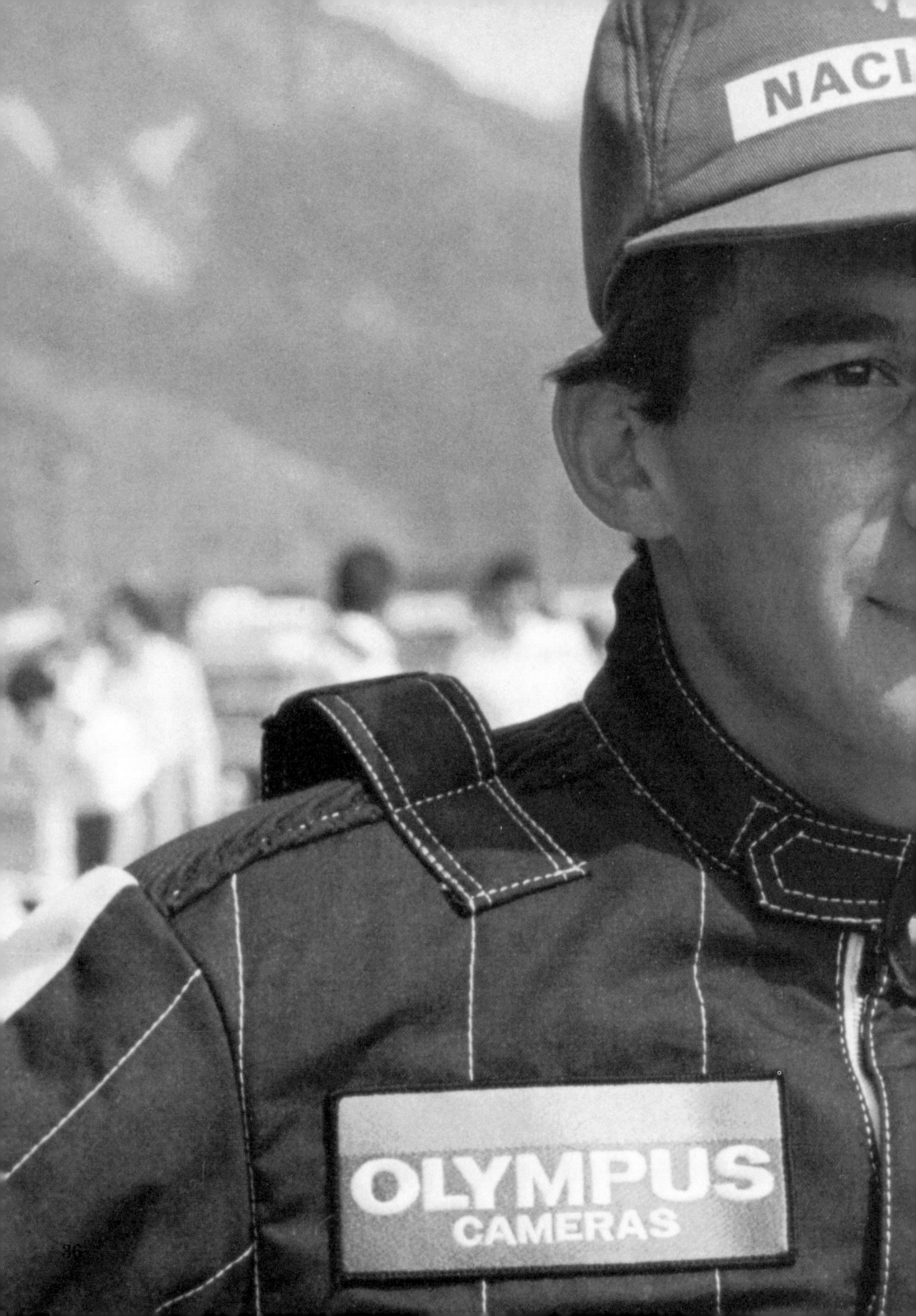
NACI
OLYMPUS
CAMERAS

The most outstanding
new talent to arrive on
the Grand Prix scene in
recent years has
undoubtedly been Ayrton
Senna, the young
Brazilian driver who
switched from Toleman
to Lotus at the start of the
1985 season. I feel that
Senna's skill is of a type
seen only rarely in
Formula 1; he clearly has
an extremely bright
future.

When I got the opportunity to move into Formula 1 in 1965, I had three offers to consider and I finally decided that my prospects would be best served by joining Graham Hill at BRM. As these photographs suggest, we quickly established an informal, often lighthearted partnership which was very valuable for me because I knew I could learn a lot from him without being under too much pressure to produce results too quickly. BRM turned out to have been precisely the right choice and although I personally felt rather uncomfortable when I began running as quickly as Graham, he never showed any signs of holding that against me.

40

own ability. You must absolutely discipline yourself never to go beyond that point. That's where the 'clinical' criticism comes in. People say 'why didn't he go for it?' When I went off the road early in 1985 in the new four-wheel drive Ford RS200 prototype I was testing on the Boreham Special Stage, I should probably have stopped one lap before I went off. I had it in my mind to do it, but I made the wrong decision. I was doing that last lap because I wanted to learn more about the car's behaviour, but if, in fact, I'd been a little brighter I'd have realised that I wasn't going to make any more progress. The tyres had already 'gone off', so the chassis was no longer giving me good information.

I didn't live with my own judgement, and I know it. It didn't cost me much, but it reminded me of a good lesson. One of the reasons I'm sitting here today is that I generally lived well by my own initiative, by my own judgement, about stopping before I did something silly. Or before elements or circumstances caused something untoward to occur. Sometimes it's difficult to take the bull by the horns and make a good clear judgement. You'll be given more credit for stopping early than stopping late. And when you are driving over your limits, something will happen; OK, with the Ford I just broke a bit of fibreglass, but it could have been worse, just as easily. There was no point in it, so I broke my own rule.

I can't remember ever having broken my own rule like that when I was in F1. I remember stopping more often than I remember continuing. I never did, for example, one more lap than I needed to do at the old Nürburgring in Germany. It's 14 miles (23km) round, has about 180 corners per lap and was the world's most difficult and possibly most dangerous track. There were so many occasions when I was over the limit because it required a commitment early on in a sequence of corners. Once you get started into them at that pace, that trajectory, you didn't stop half-way through. From *Brunchen* there was a section like that; the descent to *Adenau*; the *Foxhole* and up through the left- and right-hander at the end of it; the *Haztenbach* section. There were so many sections of the Nürburgring where you were just a passenger, although perhaps I was slightly less of a passenger than some other people. I knew that I was going at a speed that if anything ever so slightly went wrong there was no space to get out of the trouble; I mean I was going to have a mammoth accident. I never did a single lap more at the Nürburgring than I had to, never. I never enjoyed it when I was there; I enjoyed it in January or February in front of a log fire, or talking about how I did it. But, no, I didn't enjoy the place when I was there.

OK, so you ask, 'What about your win in 1968?' I had tyres which were a great help to me that day, but so did Piers Courage and one or two other drivers. But that wasn't the point. That day I drove well, took the advantage at the right time, even though I didn't start from the front of the grid. But don't make any mistakes about the fact that I wouldn't have wanted to do one more lap. You've got to know where to stop. Never drive outside your limitations.

Chapter 2
The Formative Years

Let's consider those crucially important formative years, the early years when somebody has been given the freedom to use the road for the very first time after receiving their driving licence. In the same vein we can also examine the problems and pitfalls in front of the novice competitor as he faces his first taste of competition motoring: they are part and parcel of the same thing.

The early years of one's career are, of course, the formative ones although, paradoxically, to begin with they are not effectively very formative. The experiences are so overwhelming there is no room in your mind for shaping opinions or techniques, only space for soaking up all that experience and living that experience. Just to have the freedom of the car and the road, to be able to drive, to pilot your own destiny if you like, is still an adventure for any young person. For anybody to shrug it off as 'well, it's no big deal' is just deprecatory. They are merely trying to be impressive and macho, but when they got out for the first time without another driver sitting beside them, without L-plates, I don't know anybody who hasn't experienced a sense of thrill and exhilaration, with the feeling of freedom and independence simply by being in that position of command. But they can be dangerous years.

We all start out without any experience or knowledge. We have been back-seat drivers, in effect, from the time we were children and sat with our parents and seen them shouting at people and people shouting at them. We've always been a third party: it's either been amusing or embarrassing, but it's been somebody else's problem. It hasn't been ours. But now it is suddenly our problem and we just haven't got the experience. We're fed up with our mother, our father, our driving instructor telling us 'for God's sake be careful. Don't do this, don't do that, have you done this, have you done that. Have you looked across the road, have you looked behind that bus, have you got your lights dipped . . .'

You end up wondering 'why are they telling me all these things? Don't tell me I'm going too fast; I'm not going too fast'. But at this early stage, you don't have enough miles on the clock to come to the correct conclusion that you are going too fast. You don't know that you are going too fast for the limited talent that you have accumulated at that time. Talent is not simply turning the steering wheel, it includes underlying knowledge and you cannot gain that knowledge without experience.

It is my personal view, and I know it is not shared by everybody, that nobody should get themselves into racing before having gained considerable mileage on the road. The reason for that is because the simplest and

The young driver on the road has a great deal to think about and assimilate in his early years. There is absolutely no substitute for experience, for miles under one's belt, and the novice will necessarily be most vulnerable simply because he has not accumulated a fund of knowledge on which to draw. It is of paramount importance that a young driver should appreciate the implications of his inexperience and tread a cautious path.

basic lessons are learned by spending time behind the wheel in a racing car, but even if your name is Getty, the racing car doesn't run long enough. The racing teams don't have sufficient cars, or engines, or wheels, or tyres, to give unlimited time on a circuit. A few hundred miles of running on a race track is a mammoth amount in racing terms, but it's tiny compared with the possibility of doing 50,000 miles in a year on the road. And through those 50,000 miles, through those four seasons perhaps, you would be able to gain experience in rain, snow and ice, poor visibility, arid conditions, slippery leaves in autumn. You will experience other people doing things to you which will alert you to risks which you never ever thought existed – risks which don't just happen on the race track, but also happen on the road.

One of my sons had an accident early in his road driving experience, a small accident in the snow and ice. He came down a steep hill, locked up the wheels, slid gently over a T-junction and hit another car a glancing blow. Poor Paul was just sitting there watching all this happen, with his mother sitting beside him, because he didn't know what to do. He had had his driving licence for less than a year. If it had been his father he probably wouldn't have done that. But he wasn't in first gear in the automatic Mercedes G-wagon's box, he was in drive. He didn't have anti-lock brakes, so he locked up. Of course he tried to steer it away from the collision but with the wheels locked it went straight on. But, worse still, after being left sitting in the middle of the junction, he was now parked in the middle of the road, he reversed back to get out of the way, straight into a lamp post, doing more damage to my G-wagon than he had initially hitting the guy who was going up the road.

He made that second mistake because he was so flustered, through inexperience, reversing into that lamp post! It was 'Oh my God, I've crashed my father's car, I've hit another car, now I'm blocking the road. I must get out of the way. And thump!'

Now, Paul is a very good driver, but he was inexperienced at that time. Had he been more experienced, maybe the first accident would not have happened. But, for the purposes of this discussion, let's assume that, even with extraordinary knowledge and experience, that accident would have happened. He would have then looked up and down the road, realised that the other car was OK, realised nobody was going to hit him because the road was clear and thought out clearly what he was going to do next. It would have given a beat before the next movement. You can't get that clarity of logical thought without experience.

Paul learned from that accident. Then, about a month later, he had another accident, this time in America, at the wheel of his own car, a four-wheel drive Bronco 2. In snowy conditions again, he went round a corner and it just wouldn't steer; he slid right across the road in the path of anything that might have been coming the other way and he ran into one of those wire hawser barriers. Of course, he damaged the car – not badly, but it cost a thousand dollars to fix and it was his accident.

He was embarrassed to tell me about it. I asked him 'Paul, were you going too fast?' He said, 'No, I wasn't going too fast.' I replied, 'OK, so you weren't going too fast. But how did you go across the road, across the line of any potential oncoming traffic and run into the opposite barrier if you weren't going too fast? You were obviously going too fast for the conditions.'

He had to acknowledge that it was the case. Despite two painful experiences, his nightmare isn't over. He was 19 years of age at the time and he's going to make more mistakes. He'll get over that initial feeling of inadequacy he felt after that second accident. The next thing might well be a dry weather accident which is going to be a faster accident. You only hope that somebody that young, with that little experience, is going to learn from minor incidents instead of the most awful accident which we all know can happen on the road.

Very few people reading this chapter will have any concept of the kind of energies involved in coming into contact with either another vehicle, or a solid object, while driving a motor car, never mind a 200 mph accident at Indianapolis or Monza. I'm talking about a 30/40 mph accident on the streets of Europe or America. But when somebody has an accident like this, and they've been lectured by their parents to be careful, it's not the damage to the car their parents are worried about. Of course, they're concerned about the expense, the no-claims bonus and the inconvenience, but it's their children's lives they are worried about in the end.

Young people don't understand – and I'm not talking down to them in any way – that if you hit a solid object at 30 mph, even in a well-built, safety-conscious car, the impact is the same as jumping out of the third storey of a building onto a concrete floor. That's fact.

If anyone thinks they can survive that kind of thing at 40-50-60 mph, *they are wrong!* Without dwelling on the safety and the wearing of seat belts, for example, it is absolutely imperative that we all recognise this kind of situation. Yet, when the adrenalin pumps and the thrill and desire surfaces, that kind of statistic gets buried.

But it would be very wrong of us not to identify this sort of problem. So, whether it might be an oncoming vehicle that Paul could have struck while in America on the snow – to think about it even makes my goose-pimples rise – or a correspondingly precarious situation on a race track in competitive conditions, we must appreciate how this problem of youth and inexperience prevents a driver from making an accurate judgement of the speed he is doing in a certain specific situation.

The next point is that it is almost impossible to think much while driving when you are that young and inexperienced. You are driving by the seat of your pants. You have got to accommodate that talent without over-driving, without going over the top of your head. That, again, is trying to discipline yourself into not overstepping the limits of yourself and your car. In the case of changing weather conditions – always a factor in Europe when you can suddenly find yourself driving in the rain – just keep in mind just how much more slippery it is than in the dry. If you start to get it wrong and the car doesn't respond you can go onto the grass, into banks, into barriers . . . you really need to be aware of all this.

Our enthusiasm for driving should be tempered. Driving a car for the first time is a marvellous fulfilment. To handle it correctly, to balance it, to control the car as you sweep through a series of curves is uniquely satisfying. But if the slightest mistake is made it can be a major drama. It's far worse than missing a tennis ball, or slicing a golf shot, or missing the basket in basketball or missing the penalty kick. The implications are absolutely enormous, not only in terms of physical damage but also mechanical damage.

You have to see driving as it really is. Don't get any false impressions that you can walk on water – or that a small accident is no big deal.

Young racing drivers have an added complication to their life, in a way that other sportsmen do not. When you play tennis, you are usually alone on the court, unless you are playing doubles when your partner is on your side of the net – and he's not likely to run into you deliberately. When you are driving any kind of competition car, you are dealing with hostile competitors who want the same piece of track as you. If there is only one line at Paddock Bend at Brands Hatch, or through *Signes* at Paul Ricard, they want that same line. My advice to young drivers is that they should get experience at a racing driver's school. That is quite important. If one of my sons wanted to go racing I would send him to a racing driver's school, just to get experience and miles on a variety of different types of vehicles.

Having said that, if he wanted to go racing, I would like him to get his first year's experience in a fully enclosed touring car, with enclosed wheels and a roll cage. Since you are young and since you are inexperienced, you will unquestionably make mistakes. If you make mistakes in close company coming off the starting grid in an open-wheeled single-seater car, you can interlock wheels. That interlocking effect, due to the turning motion of the wheel, is like engaging a gear and it can throw a car up into the air. This kind of accident can be enormous because the driver is so vulnerable in a single-seater. Lives can be lost. And there are, sadly, some former racing drivers, now paraplegics, who never had the benefit of learning by mistakes in single-seater cars. The penalty can be much greater than in a fully enclosed and protected touring car. In a touring car the novice might collide with another competitor, spin off, hit the odd bank, he may even turn over, but it's unlikely that it will be the end of the line. So I think this is a good category for a novice driver to start in.

Equally, as a novice, the young driver may recognise deficiencies in circuit safety which are not apparent to more senior drivers accustomed to the layout of most circuits, and whose level of skill makes it unnecessary to consider as hazardous certain features which could threaten drivers at a

lower level of experience. A young driver who is aware of his personal safety and his racing future should not be timid about making suggestions for the improvement of circuit safety or paddock facilities of which he has personal experience.

Young drivers should never use less than the very best equipment when it comes to driver protection. Don't buy a cheap helmet, buy the best. It's at this stage that you need the best; you need less as you become less of a risk to yourself. If you damage a helmet, if you drop it, have it checked. Don't treat it as if it was just a piece of junk. Wrap your helmet up in a nice felt bag – you might get one with a new helmet if you buy a good make. Ensure that the walls of the helmet bag are protected. Look after your helmet as if it was a piece of jewellery: it's one of the most valuable things you'll ever own because it's going to protect the most vulnerable part of your body.

I can never understand people who treat their helmets badly although even some top line racing drivers seem to do so. My helmet is an important part of my business. I had my own identification on it and I always wanted to keep it immaculate. I polished my own helmet. I had pride in its appearance. Helen might clean it up after a race, but I would always go over the helmet and polish it up, because if I did that I would see whether it had picked up any marks which it hadn't got before. I saw that the visor was clipped in properly. I did all of that myself: it's part of my preparation, just as I clean my own gun. That way I know all the little details – and if I'm not attending to that kind of detail, how on earth can I expect other people to attend to it. The helmet could have a slight crack in it, the inner lining could be coming out, the strap could be dislodged.

I never kept a helmet for more than a year. I always thought that perhaps

The congested road environment can be quite daunting to young drivers. Not only have they to master the mechanics of handling a car, but they are pitched into this jungle of vehicles, road signs, traffic lights and restrictions. I always emphasise to young people that they should drive well within their capabilities.

For the competition driver life can become precarious, as the Metro vaulting the Thruxton chicane clearly indicates. I think it is a good idea for a novice to opt for a saloon car in which to begin a competition career. If you end up on your roof it may be expensive in financial terms but you probably won't do yourself any serious personal harm.

48

49

Ambitious youngsters
who want to go all the
way to Grand Prix racing
will almost certainly
have gained karting or
Formula Ford experience
at some stage in their
career, but this junior
single-seater category is
ferociously competitive
at every level. The
photograph of Bertrand
Gachot launching himself
into orbit during the 1985
Formula Ford Festival at
Brands Hatch is a good
reminder of how
suddenly cars running in
close company can
become embroiled in an
accident. It goes without
saying that good quality
safety equipment is a
number one priority.

somebody could have dropped it. Perhaps the baggage handler at Heathrow has damaged it. In reality, a truck could have run it over for all I knew. So I replaced it regularly.

Let's talk about overalls. Don't wear racing underwear without normal underwear underneath. And buy thermal underwear which is too big – don't get something which looks as if it should be on a tailor's dummy. Air is the best insulator, and you can't have air inside underwear or a suit which is too tight. It's a great temptation to look chic inside skin-tight overalls, but they won't protect you so well.

So wear cotton underwear, then wear thermal underwear – too big – then get your overalls – too big. Never wear anything under other than good quality thermal socks – I always wore two pairs. I wore two sets of thermal underwear too, but most people don't want to do that. Wear a balaclava. You won't like it, it will be uncomfortable and initially you may find it difficult to breathe through. But wear it. One day it may save your life.

Early on, if you can afford it, put a medical air supply into your helmet, whatever your car is, whether it be a single-seater or a touring car. Very few people die from burns, very few indeed. They died from inhalation of flame, smoke, toxic fumes or heat. So if you've got a full-face helmet with a piped air supply, you'll have an additional 45 to 60 seconds of air. You may be unconscious, but you'll be breathing medical air which doesn't burn, not oxygen which does. If you're not rescued in a minute or so in a major fire you're probably going to die anyway because your overalls and thermal underwear are not going to last longer than that.

This is a reflection of your attitude; not only to your family and the people who care for you, but to the mechanics. They will see you going to that kind of trouble for your personal protection, so they will become infected by the same attention to detail in their work on your behalf. It is infectious, unquestionably. Start off by doing all the right things. Wear the best gloves: I always wore Bury and Hopwood gloves made by a nice man in the Midlands who is a member of the Worshipful Company of Glove Makers. He makes a good product out of best quality materials and is always interested. Gloves are very important. Don't start with the pair your mother or your aunt gave you for Christmas that are made of thin leather. They're more like golf gloves: they feel nice, but if you should ever end up in a fire with them they'll frizzle up and just melt. The palm of your hand cannot be brought back. The backs of your hands are a little easier. No plastic surgeon today can give you good hands if the palms have been badly burnt. The palm is very difficult to repair.

So kit yourself out correctly. I know it is expensive. But, if I was a young up-and-coming driver, I would far rather have all my Christmas and birthday presents from all my relations to add to my equipment than have a cheap kit. Also, have them laundered regularly, because that will be seen as another example of your own personal attention to detail. If you look right, you start regarding these factors as important and, in the same way, other people see you regarding these factors as worthwhile. It is a significant image builder.

Having created the image take every opportunity to identify your own name with it. A driver's name should appear on his helmet, helmet bag and luggage, overalls, his racing car and any courtesy cars or transporters he uses. Everything identified with that driver should have his name very much in evidence – it all helps to establish and enhance his reputation and image.

When you begin driving, a lot of the mechanics you will be dealing with

I do not believe that accidents should be dwelt on, but all competitors ought to be aware of the forces involved in even relatively minor impacts. This photograph of Philippe Alliot's RAM Formula 3000 car against the barrier at Silverstone during an off-season testing accident is a reminder of what can happen. In this case, the car's energy was dissipated as suspension components and side pods were broken, and the driver was able to walk away. But a head-on impact into an immovable object at much lower speeds can have far more serious personal consequences.

will be just as inexperienced as you are. Some of them may have been around a few more years, but in general the very fact that they are in that level of the sport suggests that they might not have a great deal of experience. They may well make mistakes, as we all can.

Take part in the preparation of your own car as much as you can. You may not have sat your City and Guilds Certificate in Motor Engineering, but it doesn't matter! You know that there is a thing called a torque wrench, which can tighten bolts up to a certain setting rather than strip them by going too tight. You can learn how to wire up components – simple things like the oil cap and the water cap. Then, if you walk round and check these things, the mechanics will be impressed that you've gone to the trouble. Walk round and make sure that there are valve caps on all the wheels. If dirt gets into that valve, it can deflate your tyre at any time, and all because of lack of attention.

Young drivers can gain a better understanding of basic techniques from a course at a racing drivers' school, such as Brands Hatch Racing and Jim Russell's school at Snetterton (above). Chief Instructor John Kirkpatrick is seen, left, briefing new drivers. Bob Bondurant's High Performance school at Sears Point offers similar benefits to road drivers.

If anybody has been working on the car, go to the trouble of looking round the cockpit to make sure no tools are lying there and, particularly, the footwell. As I recount in rather more detail in a later section of this book (The High Performance Technique), I had a very nasty moment testing a Tyrrell Formula 2 Matra at Goodwood when a spanner left in the footwell jammed the brake off and the throttle pedal open. It's not something I want to think about too much, even now, and it's something that a novice should guard against being exposed to at all costs!

It's an easy mistake to make. Working all night in the garage, the paddock, at home . . . it can happen. And for a driver to look round is no disrespect to the mechanic: in fact, he'll be glad that you did it. That is part of the preparation of being a conscientious driver and competitor.

Looking back on my first full season as a Grand Prix driver, with BRM back in 1965, the only area in which I had the capacity to make any reasonable technical comment was something as simple as rollbar adjustment: whether I wanted more roll stiffness at the front or the rear. But, if I was doing it all again, I would make certain I knew rather more of the technicalities and implications of those changes before I progressed as far as I had by the start of that first F1 season.

It takes time before you can come in and discuss in detail with your mechanics precisely what needs to be done, to identify the precise adjustments that need to be made. A young driver needs to find out very early in his career what the effect of changing springs and adjusting rollbars actually is. This is a matter which we discuss in more detail in 'The High Performance Technique', but the point needs to be underlined here simply because a novice driver will probably only have a 20 minute practice session at many club events during which time he not only has to set up the car correctly, but often learn the circuit. And who can afford to have days and days of private testing at this stage in their career?

It is not like a tennis player who can stand up and practise against a wall, or even use a ball machine, or a golfer at a driving range. So practice, as such, doesn't come into play so much for a young racing driver. And that is why it takes longer for a young driver to mature than a young tennis player. Take Mats Wilander winning the French Open at, what was he, 17 years old? It is difficult to imagine the motor racing equivalent – a 17-year old winning a Grand Prix – ever taking place.

It took me three years from my start in racing before I got into Formula 1 – and that was quick. I don't think that happens very often and, indeed, I believe that it should take longer because, quite frankly, there is just too much to learn. I don't think we, the motor racing community, in fact govern this part of our activities too well. It's only fifty years or so since the driving test was made compulsory, but I do feel that we should concentrate very carefully on the way in which we allow people to progress through such a demanding and challenging sport as ours.

Racing miles are *absolutely* crucial. I'm in favour of a young driver's performance being monitored in detail and an upgrading system which would depend on experience. By that I mean racing miles, completing races over a certain distance. The importance of time on the track is something that cannot be underestimated, but as I have said, I have major reservations about drivers going into racing before they've ever held a driving licence. Karting certainly helps in terms of racecraft, as has been proved by people like Ronnie Peterson, Emerson Fittipaldi, Stefan Johansson and a host of others.

I got my son to go to Bob Bondurant's high performance school – rather

When buying a helmet it is worth getting the highest quality product you can afford. And look after it very carefully indeed! Avoid dropping it and check regularly for any minor crack damage which might impair its protective qualities. Keeping it in a lined helmet bag should help to protect it from inadvertent knocks and scratches. When choosing gloves, don't fall into the trap of thinking that 'any old gloves' will do. You should be buying specialised kit for a specialised purpose.

56

than a pure racing school – because it is orientated towards road driving. I think it is beneficial to do this before contemplating a racing drivers' course, if you can afford it. Maybe I'm overdoing the cautious aspect, but it's not like playing tennis or playing golf. There are just so many potential risks and pitfalls involved.

Keep in mind, of course, that, in my opinion, it is not imperative to be totally involved at a particularly young age as far as racing cars is concerned. I didn't drive a racing car until I was 23 years of age. There's no rush to get started. It's not a sport in which youth necessarily plays a crucial role. The fact that Mike Thackwell was the youngest driver ever to start a Grand Prix, that Jody Scheckter hoped to be the youngest Grand Prix winner, that Emerson Fittplaid turned out to be the youngest ever World Champion . . . that's all unimportant. It's a record which nobody really should care about.

What is more important, and impressive, is for a team manager to see some maturity coming out from his potential driver. The team manager is going to think 'yes, I'll have him because he's going to be just that little bit more together. The younger lad is going to cost me more in accident repairs and cause me trouble . . .' I would far rather a youngster goes steadily through this preparatory programme. If you want to go racing, get organised in club level karting, a very healthy sport. Get your racecraft organised. Have fun. But go about it in an organised way.

This early experience also perhaps gives you the opportunity of learning to attract sponsors for the first time. You will discover how to deal with them, how to coax them, to give them value for money. Be ambitious, of course, but don't think you've got to be in Formula 3 by the age of 21 or you're going to be a dead man. You're more likely to be a dead man – literally – when you're 19 through lack of experience . . .

Having said that, motor racing is a fast-moving sport in which a driver needs to keep his name in the limelight. After the initial promise and progress my career produced through 1965 and 1966, the rules governing Formula 1 changed and I found myself racing the uncompetitive BRM H16 during 1967 which made me worry a little about my prospects. I began to wonder whether I would ever be able to get back into a top-line team, or would I just face life simply as a run-of-the-mill driver.

So I went off to drive Formula 2 quite a lot in an effort to keep my name in the limelight for other people's benefit. So that they might say, 'Well, that H16 isn't going too well, but that lad's keeping up with the front runners in F2, so he can't be too bad.' People are either in love with you or they ignore you completely. If they start ignoring you, there's the chance that you'll stop getting breaks and no longer have the decent drives.

There is always an anxious new talent standing on the sidelines keen to take your place in the team, intent on making a name for himself. So it is a good thing for a driver to race as much as he possibly can in other categories, particularly if his major single-seater programme is not bringing him much good luck.

Despite the fact that the H16 BRM had been so troublesome in 1967, Ferrari and Ken Tyrrell were both keen to have me for 1968, while BRM was anxious to keep hold of me with promises for the future. People still wanted me to drive for them, but this was only because I had shown my prowess in other categories such as Formula 2 and sports cars. Had I not moved into other categories to demonstrate my talent, who knows what might have happened?

It was a frustrating time, not too depressing, but the H16 was a heavy, cumbersome car: it didn't matter who you were, it would just lap at a certain speed. I drove it, Chris Irwin drove it, Mike Spence drove it: the other two were as fast as I was and there was no way in which I could raise it above that performance plateau. The car just bogged you down. It wasn't an exciting car to drive at all.

There was a stage in the mid-1970s when people used to feel that if you were not in F1 by the time you're 24 it was all over bar shouting. That's rubbish!

I also firmly believe that an alternative form of sport can be useful. I was lucky when I started, having been involved in another sport. I had another activity because I wanted to be *somebody* within my own family. My brother was a racing driver and it seemed to me, looking back, that everything in the family was geared towards him. I wanted to be good at something. I'd not been good at school and I wasn't really outstanding at home. So I took up shooting to prove myself, which may have had something to do with my mental make-up.

I was a disaster at school, really. Only wnen I was over 40 years of age did I find out that I was suffering from dyslexia. None of my teachers ever acknowledged it, or recognised it, and consequently never treated it in a manner that might have helped. In those days, of course, it was something of an unknown quantity. I had to stay on an extra year to sit my 11-plus. And when I sat my 11-plus I got a 'C' – and there was only an 'A', 'B', 'C' and 'D'. To this day I'm a poor speller and a terribly slow reader. I can't recite the alphabet, for example – I don't know it!

I think these inabilities at school gave me a determination to succeed because amongst my peers I'd been shown up, to be so pretty damned thick – at a time when schooling was such a very central, essential part of your life. I left school at the age of 15, served petrol in a garage for a year – and earned more in the way of tips than I did from my wages – but I ran the best forecourt in the county. Then I went into the lubrication bay, and I made sure you could eat your breakfast off the floor. That was good experience.

When I started my shooting at the age of 14, I was suddenly provided with something at which I could excel. The first shoot I ever did was near Loch Lomond, on New Year's Day and I won first place. Big cup, lovely trophy. Now, whether it was my wonderful skill or whether everybody was so intoxicated on New Year's Day in Scotland, I'll never know. Nevertheless, I won the trophy, which gave me a tremendous start and enthusiasm to press on.

I went on to shoot for Scotland and then for Britain. Those years were enormously important for the information of my thinking process in dealing with competition, in dealing with success and dealing with failure. Trap shooting is a highly disciplined sport. I was lucky as I didn't smoke. I don't know whether smoking has anything to do with eyesight or reflexes but I know that drink has. Although I drink wine and champagne now, I never drank when I was racing. Nor did I drink spirits, beer, gin and tonics, or bacardi and cokes. These were what you were pushed into drinking by your peers, because it was expected of you socially. Fortunately, I had the resolve and felt confident enough in myself not to need to drink to be one of the lads.

This is something which exerts tremendous influence and pressure on young people today, whether it's through drink or through drugs. It's tough, because if you are part of a group there is an influence within that group to share your social activities. Abstinence takes strength of character. At a young age I realised that if I drank it would have a serious

Progress in the
development of fire-
resistant racing overall
has been quite remark-
able through the past
decade. Again, go for the
best quality products
available. My personal
preference was for suits
which were bigger than I
really needed as these
paid dividends in terms of
personal comfort and
allowed me to wear two
sets of flame-resistant
underwear beneath
them. Although tight
clothing may look
fashionable remember
that the more air that
circulates between the
layers of material the
greater the insulation
provided.

effect on my reflexes. If a young driver on my team who was looking to impress me stood up and asked for an orange juice, he wouldn't get any static from me.

Another sport helps you to get acclimatised to winning, to accept defeat. And that's important, because you're going to be beaten right, left and centre on your way up through motor racing, and the sooner you accept that, acknowledge it publicly, the better you're going to be as a person. People say you can't be a good loser: sure, you shouldn't be a comfortable loser and of course you're upset if you haven't done well enough. But you should know, if you are beaten, that a better man has won on that day – and you must acknowledge that.

I wasn't a bad loser: I got a lot of experience in it! In trap shooting I was thrilled if I won, or was even in the first three. But there was a time, when I got pretty good at trap shooting, that I genuinely thought I was God's gift to the sport. I was younger than the others doing it, and coming up very quickly. Then I had a very bad patch; I couldn't string a good run together. It was a good lesson, and I think the lessons that I learned from shooting had an enormous amount to do with my attitude to success in motor racing. I wasn't intoxicated by it. I honestly don't recall a period during my racing career when I was big-headed. Other people may have observed it, but I don't recall it. I do remember it in shooting, though, and I'm ashamed of that.

I see drivers who've won the World Championship in recent years getting cocky. I watch with a certain degree of amusement, because I've won three Championships and I do remember all the elements involved. I see them doing it and I think 'Oh, look a little further forward. Look a little further than you're seeing and understand how you appear to others.' My father always used to have a great saying: 'see yourself as others see you' and it's worth remembering, because sometimes you can lose sight of yourself.

I don't care how old you become, you sometimes make a slip. But that's what experience does for you and that's why another sport is of benefit. Nelson Piquet was a good tennis player before he came into racing. And I'm sure that was a benefit for him, helping to make him a better, more rounded, more mature driver much earlier than he might otherwise have been. Alain Prost was a good soccer player; I'm sure that helped.

Keep in mind that you won't be using this as a stepping stone for your racing. All that I've spoken about might sound as though the life I've enjoyed has been part of a specially structured process. That is not the case. Everything I've done in my life has, in fact, been spontaneous. A lot of people don't think it was that way, even now. They thought 'Jackie Stewart's doing this because he knows it's good for him', but it was not like that at all.

Arnold Palmer, for example, didn't create Arnie's Army. Arnie's Army created Arnie's Army, he just followed on and it became a cult. When I started, I was fairly flamboyant. It wasn't because I thought that was the image I should take up, it was simply that long hair and bell-bottomed trousers were a trend of the time. It just so happened that I went with the trend and, as a consequence, was identified with that trend.

Then, when the commercial aspect began to develop, people thought, 'Jackie Stewart's deliberately positioning himself in a way which will be advantageous for him'. That's not true. I recognised that, in some areas, there were certain things I *ought* to do – dressing, for example, in a manner consistent with the surroundings that I might be exposed to – but that doesn't mean that it was all calculated in a planned way.

Try to take an active part in the preparation of your car from an early stage in your competition career. Not only will you be increasing your technical knowledge, but also the mechanics working on the car will regard you with increased respect and are likely to respond with an extra effort.

60

On one occasion, when I was on my way to a meeting with Goodyear, I caught sight of myself in a mirror and went straight back to my hotel room where I changed into a suit. That was the right decision because people remember. It's important to recognise what other people notice. Don't assume that because you're a racing driver you can come in in tennis shoes and jeans . . .

That company you're dealing with is going to take you on and you're going to be its ambassador – you're going to carry its name everywhere you go. If the main decision-makers are uncomfortable with you for projecting the image of their company, then they might not decide to use you. Or, if they do have you, it might only be on a short-term basis. So changing that

Me shooting, Nigel Mansell golfing: both cases reinforce the point that a driver who excels in motor sport tends to be proficient in other areas. Not only are other sports a relaxing counterpoint to the business of Grand Prix racing, they can also help to keep you sharp and in trim physically, while at the same time they provide an outlet for a competitive spirit in a completely different environment.

sports jacket to a suit just might have been a small factor which helped me to have a relationship with the Goodyear Tire and Rubber Company fifteen years later. That's a long time in a commercial relationship. And if I go to a Ford Motor Company function, where perhaps I'll be travelling with the Chairman of the Board in a corporate jet, I'll be more conservatively turned out than he will. I have to be, because people will expect me *not* to be – perhaps they'll expect me to still be wearing racing overalls!

That relationship with Ford started in 1964, and there has not been a year since then when I haven't been related to, or had a contract with, that company. That relationship, under contract, will go on until 1988 – and hopefully beyond that.

But why have I been so long with those companies? Because we've been good together, because I, hopefully, have given them value for money. I hope I've given them more than they've given me. If I hadn't, they wouldn't have continued with me.

Dressed for business. From an early stage in my career I believed that it was crucially important to be dressed correctly for the occasion, whether this was in or out of the cockpit. I think it is a mistake to believe that large commercial organisations will indulge casual dress in a sportsman they wish to be associated with. If you need a sponsor or want someone to become involved with a business venture, then help yourself by dressing appropriately.

In the mid-Seventies James Hunt and Niki Lauda brought an air of casual informality to the Grand Prix scene, but it is my feeling that they went too far in projecting this sort of image. Nobody would dispute the fact that they are individualists, but there were probably instances when they did not do themselves any favours by being so casually attired.

Strapped into the cockpit of the Team Surtees Lola T70 at Mosport Park, Canada, late 1965. The car is being worked on by Surtees himself (left) shortly before he was involved in a serious accident in a similar T70. My outings in this big V8-engined sports racing car provided me with much-needed additional experience early in my career, emphasising the desirability of gaining as much mileage behind the wheel in as great a variety of cars as possible.

All I can do is hand this information to younger competitors coming along. Other people have done it different ways, but there are not many of them around, and not many of them earning big money. It's not just a question of saying it's an image factor but involves putting yourself in a position where people respect you.

I'll give you an example. Quite recently I attended a club meeting in France and suggested to Ford France that it would be a good idea if I walked round the paddock and had my photograph taken with each of the Formula Ford drivers present, perhaps to help them and their sponsors. During the course of that tour, I saw the drivers who were obviously not going to make it, some who had a slight chance and a very few who had the right idea.

You could judge this by the preparation of their cars, the attitudes of the mechanics, the knowledge that I was coming round and the way in which they set up their whole équipe for the photograph. Three or four did it half-way decently out of a field of thirty; and that was the final of the French FF Championship, so that thirty represented the top level of that particular class.

There is no excuse for a Formula Ford club driver to appear on the starting grid in a car which is anything less than absolutely spick and span. I don't want to see any dirt inside any road wheel, or any exhaust pipe which is not blacked, or any cylinder block with oil leaking down it. You don't have to be a skilled engineer to clean it . . .

When I was preparing other people's cars, I was really fussy about that preparation: that's how I got my chance. I got it because Barry Filer, the man whose cars I was preparing, had to give up because his family wouldn't allow him to race. He had an AC Bristol and a Porsche Super 90 and they were prepared at our garage. You could have eaten your dinner off any part of that AC, I can tell you. The insides of the wheel arches were wax polished, every wire wheel was cleaned, the tyres were blacked inside and out. He was so impressed over the hours I put in that he gave me a drive in a sprint at Heathfield, near Ayr, in the Porsche Super 90.

It's interesting the way in which drivers' dress styles have evolved. Before the war people like Dick Seaman, Carraciola and their colleagues were usually immaculately dressed, while, after the war, we had characters such as Ascari, with his powder blue short-sleeved shirts and matching trousers, Hawthorn with his bow tie, then Moss and Clark who were always smartly turned out in their Dunlop overalls. Fangio's dress style was modest, even down to having an unobtrusively coloured helmet, but he, like the others, was always very cleanly turned out. He was not at all pretentious, but he was still smart.

I like to think that I took enough trouble to look smart, but after I retired we entered the anti-establishment era. Emerson Fittipaldi was always smart enough, but Niki Lauda and James Hunt got together as pals: James in shorts and no shoes, Niki in an open-neck shirt and courduroys. It was always tacky, but then it became the vogue to look like that. Jacques Laffite came along in a similar way: it was smart to down-dress. I never agreed with that.

If you talk about success – commercial success, or advancing your career which is dependent on financial support – then you've got to take stock of yourself and decide what you want to be. If you want to be Mr Careless Casual, then don't expect big companies to support you, because they won't. The bigger the company, the more conservative it's likely to be and the more concern it is going to pay to the image that you may project by having any association with that company's symbol.

Truly my formative years! Photographed with my father in 1962 during my trap shooting heyday.

When I go to Goodyear at Akron, I wouldn't wear a coloured shirt. I wear a white shirt. Out of respect and regard for the surroundings. It's nothing to do with trying to be somebody that I'm not. It's a question of carrying your nameplate with you, and the name of people who have chosen to be associated with you, and if you behave in a manner that is unbecoming to their perception of what life is all about, then you may have a problem.

Chapter 3
The Physical Aspect

The physical aspect involved in any sport is of major consequence. Not enough emphasis is put on physical conditioning by a great many sports people: clearly, if you're a track and field, or athletic exponent, you must be in top physical condition.

But there are many sports where durability is a major issue. And in some of those sports it's not even acknowledged that the people involved are athletes. There have been many occasions, particularly in the USA, where strong arguments have been put forward against racing drivers being considered athletes at all. It is quite easy to understand why some critics would question that factor. If you look at some of the good old boys in the Southern Stock Car trail, you might ask 'now, how can a man carrying that much weight be classified as an athlete?' But then someone might have asked the same question of Alexof, the great Russian weightlifter who was, to say the least, overweight and at times you would have seen him hanging with fat. Some of the Japanese Sumo wrestlers may be incredibly strong, but they are also very fat. However, that is the particular build necessary for them to perform the function of their sport. So, in my mind, the same can be said of those Southern Stock Car drivers.

They have to sit in what is almost an oven for 500 miles. They lose extraordinary amounts of weight due to dehydration, and in their 'hot boxes' they have to use considerable physical effort to drive the cars. I've only driven a stock car for a few laps, and I can tell you that even at that time, when I was still actively driving Grand Prix cars, I was surprised at the exertion needed. I dare say that I was not doing it as efficiently as in the cockpit of a Grand Prix car, so I was probably using more energy than a stock car driver would expend, but nevertheless I was surprised by what was involved.

The Formula 1 driver is the most physically fit that I see on the car racing circuit – although the best in motorsports are in fact on motor cycles, particularly in motocross where many of the riders have fine physiques. This is because the entire body is being used, and a form of isometrics and strength exercises is being demanded of their bodies. This not only includes arms, neck, shoulder and upper body muscles, but also hips, legs and even the feet. Most of the time they are standing up on the foot rests, taking enormous punishment, needing flexibility worthy of a shock absorber in terms of vertical movement, while at the same time moving from side to side rather like the pendulum of a grandfather clock. Nobody could dispute that those men are athletes in the fullest sense of the word.

In most walks of life I don't feel enough people take sufficient time preparing their mind and their body properly. There's no doubt that physical fitness produces mental fitness. If you're physically fit, you will be more mentally alert, better able to handle the strains and stresses which can sometimes appear in modern life. They can be the result of too much work, too many problems, too many people, too many financial pressures. They can be the result of an accident or illness.

I suffered from stress during my racing career and I still do today. I'm speaking now from a mental point of view, but it also happens physically. It usually happened, while I was racing, at the end of June or the beginning of July. Then again it occurred in November. Nowadays it happens in late spring and late autumn. However, I've learned now to recognise the symptoms and prepare for the period which I know is going to be tough for me, and this is where a book such as this can be of some help to those who are just setting out on their careers. I had to find these things out through my own suffering and self-analysis. And I think that self-analysis is a very important element of any person's mental make up. Unless you are able to analyse your mind and body very clearly, you are likely to miss all sorts of important messages.

Let's deal with eyesight first of all. Funnily enough eyesight is something which I don't put a tremendous importance on. There have been many racing drivers who wear glasses. Tom Sneva, one of the fastest drivers of all time in the modern era at Indianapolis, wears glasses. Other wearers have included John Miles, a very competent driver in Europe; the late Masten Gregory, one of the fastest sports car drivers in the Fifties and early-Sixties; the late Rolf Stommelen, a GP and international sports car driver of renown. So it's not necessary to have perfect eyesight. But it is a benefit not to have to wear glasses, because of fogging, because of them coming off the bridge of your nose, and the general discomfort. Contact lenses have not been encouraged in motorsport because of the possible dangers should they become dislodged or in the event of an accident.

If there is a young driver reading this now who has been told to forget motor racing because his eyes not 20/20, then I don't think this is necessarily a correct judgement. If he is outstandingly talented, has natural ability and the right mental attitude, he can overcome the wearing of glasses quite easily. What he can't overcome, however, is to be very unfit, physically weak. One has to have a stamina factor, which is all-important. That doesn't mean of course, that you have to look like Arnold Schwarzenegger – it may please the eye on Copacabana beach if you ever get to Rio, but it's not looked upon as an attribute by people who really know in this business. It's no good being muscle-bound. I like to see people with long muscles rather than short fat muscles. If this can be achieved by exercise, and it can, then you're going to be a much better athlete, certainly to drive a racing car.

The last thing you need is weight; designers spend a lot of time and money saving weight, so you must keep your weight down. You do need good cardiovascular fitness for a number of reasons. First of all, the more oxygen consumption you have within your body, the more oxygen gets to your brain and the clearer your thinking processes become. This isn't just my own opinion, but one voiced by much more informed medical sources.

Running, very simply, for me is probably the best exercise. I exercised a lot from 1968 onwards and running was the staple diet for that training. What I didn't do, however, in those early days was to stretch correctly before and after running. If you were to watch Carl Lewis, four-times Olympic gold medallist, you would never see him simply climb out of bed in

Exhilaration: on my way to victory at Monaco in 1973, a circuit whose appeal has never ceased to fascinate me even after I retired from the cockpit.

72

continued on page 89

Formula Ford continues to be the most popular single-seater nursery formula where the relative lack of power disciplines a novice to develop a smooth style, as well as learning to work with adjustable suspension settings.

The unloved H16 – I'm just about to climb into the BRM cockpit prior to the start of the 1967 British Grand Prix at Silverstone. This car had a performance plateau beyond which it was reluctant to be pushed and it seemed to make little difference who was driving; it simply returned roughly the same results in terms of lap times. I was glad I had Formula 2 to fall back on!

During the 1967 season Formula 2 became extremely important to me as a shop window in which to display the true worth of my driving ability as I was having a hard time in Formula 1 with the BRM H16. Here is my Tyrrell-Matra MS7 battling with Jochen Rindt's Winklemann Brabham during the Formula 2 race at Rouen-les-Essarts (above).

I was never particularly at ease at the old 14-mile Nürburgring, but my victory in the rain-soaked 1968 Grand Prix was one of the most satisfying of my career (far right).

Total concentration – making a point to Ken Tyrrell (right).

78

On the grid prior to the start of the inaugural Paul Ricard French Grand Prix in 1971. I was on pole position ahead of the two Ferraris, but it was only by dint of making a really fast start that I opened a sufficient lead to prevent them slipstreaming past me in the opening stages of the race (inset).

Hurtling round Monza in one of the Cologne Capris during the 1972 European Touring Car Championship round. It was hard work on the arms for us delicate Formula 1 drivers!

81

At the wheel of Carl Haas's Lola T260 Can-Am sports racer at Watkins Glen in 1971. My enthusiasm to keep competing in an additional category led me to take on a punishing schedule that summer which eventually resulted in a stomach ulcer.

With Helen, Prince Rainier and Princess Grace on the victory rostrum after winning at Monaco in 1971. I wasn't in the best of health by this time.

Winning the French Grand Prix at Clermont-Ferrand in 1972 was particularly gratifying as it marked my return to the cockpit after six weeks at home recovering from that stomach ulcer (left).

Shaving the grass at Buenos Aires during the 1973 Argentine Grand Prix – but not dropping a wheel over the edge! (below)

**Monaco again –
winning for the last time
on my final visit there in
1973. I always felt
particularly
exhilarated after a
successful race on this
challenging circuit
(right).**

**Monza 1973, and my
third World
Championship in the
bag! Here my Tyrrell is
on the tail of Denny
Hulme's McLaren
during my climb back
through the field
following an early pit
stop (above).**

**Off duty in a relaxed
mood (overleaf).**

88

continued from page 72

the morning, pull on his shorts and singlet, put on his shoes and run down the road for five miles. He would probably stretch for 10 or 15 minutes. He would go through a process of preparation, extending his muscles, before he ever put a foot on the road inside a running shoe. And he would do the same when he finished the run, so there would be reduced danger of muscle injury due to shortening a muscle through being in bed, through lack of exercise for some hours, then suddenly having to extend that muscle through running. It need not be an Achilles tendon, the calf, or the thigh; it could be a neck muscle, a back muscle or an arm muscle. All those muscles are used when you're running.

So the warm-up is really an important element of running. This involves stretching and then going for a short run, walk, short run and walk, particularly in the beginning, and then you start off and do your running properly. I believe that all of us should take advantage of the very best advice. There are trainers who would be flattered to be asked to prepare a programme of preparation for a sport other than their own. They would then be looking in and searching for another dimension.

That trainer should be taken to a sporting event, and be shown what the body is being put through. And, of course, in short races there is not the same amount of fatigue coming into play. But the body is a strange thing: it seems to have its own timer that sets itself to almost whatever duration is required. Personally, I have quite often felt exhausted by a 20-minute spell in the car just as much as I would have been after a 12- or 24-hour race. This is because it's all a question of how much you pump out of yourself for the period required for the total performance.

Racing drivers also tend to get congested in their upper body. When they recline in a single-seated racing car, muscle tension is involved for considerable periods of time and has a way of tightening and knotting everything up, specifically the shoulders and around the neck. Wearing a crash helmet is a heavy weight to carry, which is exaggerated by the G-forces which drivers experience – whether it be the head going forward under braking or backwards under acceleration, or lateral forces in cornering. In addition to all of that you've got the jolts, the bangs and the bumps due to undulations on the circuit. So, the neck has to go through quite a lot.

Then you must consider the central nervous system which extends from the brain through the neck and down through the spine – which is not all that well supported in the case of a racing driver, certainly not in any padded form. He is usually lying in a fibreglass seat, strapped in with his vertebrae sometimes chafing against that seat. So there's not a great deal in the way of body comfort: you're not being very sympathetic to your body when you're driving a racing car.

The legs have a fair bit to do with it too, and that's where running can help because the exercise will strengthen them. In a racing car your legs are stretched out, and you may need to brace yourself because you're pulling 1½/2G in certain places.

Your feet should not be forgotten, either, because you're pressing pedals all the time. In a Grand Prix the right foot is never off the accelerator or the brake pedal. In 1965 I ran into a problem in that area which was totally unknown to me: I had to have a nerve removed from the ball of my foot because it was too close to the surface. The constant pressure inflamed the nerve to the point where it produced such pain that it was simply unbearable. It was one of the reasons why I seldom did long distance racing. Half the time I was driving with my left foot crossing over to press the

This shot of Ayrton Senna strapped tightly into his Lotus-Renault not only indicates how snug and well-supported the cockpit of a contemporary Grand Prix car actually is, but also illustrates how most drivers like a relatively upright position, close enough to the steering wheel to be able to use the full force of their arm muscles without trouble.

91

Qualities of balance and muscular co-ordination are crucially important to a racing driver, although they may not be immediately apparent to the casual onlooker. These shots of a young trials rider carefully negotiating a bumpy, rutted course gives a good visual indication of the muscular control involved in handling any competition car or motor cycle.

accelerator pedal – stretching all the way across the footwell of the car just to allow my right foot to have some relief on a long straight.

I never noticed this problem until I drove a Formula 1 car: by the end of 1965 when I did the Tasman series I was in agony. I came home from the Tasman series to have it looked at. I had to go to a brain specialist to have it fixed! Really, I'm not joking. I went into Killern Hospital in Scotland where, at that time, its main area of work was brain surgery. And mine were in my feet! The central nervous system is part of a neuro-surgeon's job. It was the nerve which was causing the problem, so it had to be cut out and blocked off. It did help, but it didn't eliminate the problem entirely. I then started to race in Hush Puppies – they must have been the fastest Hush Puppies on the market. They were thick-soled shoes and I buffed down all the corners to get them to fit properly around the pedals. I was told the half-inch thick soles would be a total disaster because in those days everybody wore paper-thin boxing boots in the interests of total sensitivity. When I began wearing these Hush Puppies it only went to confirm that I had very little sensitivity in my body – because they didn't seem to slow me down at all!

At about the same time I started to use the heavy, thick flame-proof gloves rather than the golfing gloves which the other drivers were using. Driving gloves again were supposed to be wafer-thin so you could feel every sensation in the steering wheel's feedback . . . Then, if a fire occurred, they would melt onto the palms and the backs of your hands.

That is just a terrible, unnecessary risk to take. Shopping gloves are for ladies to go shopping in, golf gloves are to play golf in . . . and racing drivers' gloves are made for a particular function, not just to give you grip on the steering wheel, but also to provide protection in the event of a fire.

To return to my feet, I was now paying extra attention to them and having them massaged. As I got into racing in a more serious way, I found that massage helped me a lot and I would have one whenever possible. It eased the congestion and tension that I would get in my neck and back. But I found only two or three people around the world who were right for my body – everybody's body reaction to massage or body treatment is different. My first experience of this was with a man called Willie Kinloch from Glasgow. He's still alive today, maturing in years and knowledge, seeming to get more aware of all the subtleties required in physical conditioning. As he gets older he sees more to be done and to be cared for. He had worked previously with football playeis, marathon runners and other athletes.

I had an accident in a BRM during the 1966 Belgian Grand Prix at Spa. I was still living in Scotland at the time and someone gave me Willie Kinloch's address. This was the first time I had met a specialist in this field and it was he who helped me back to physical condition.

Having gone through that experience, he gave me a series of exercises to try and relax with because he realised that an important element of my physical needs was based on creating the greatest amount of relaxation time. The tension that goes up your neck and upper body tends to contribute towards headaches and I used to suffer from them. He taught me that I should extend my neck, stretching the muscles. I would roll my shoulders back, then stretch my chin down as close as I could to my chest. Then I would hunch myself up, trying to get my neck inside my shoulders: then drop each shoulder in turn, down as far as it would go and move my head over to the side trying to reach the opposite shoulder, stretching again all the muscles down by my ear and down by my shoulder – really stretching and almost feeling pain.

It amounted to four basic movements. One for the back of the neck with the chin touching the chest, the second with the left shoulder stretched with the head trying to touch the right shoulder, then rolling the shoulders again and stretching the neck trying to get the back of the head to touch the back of your shoulders, stretching the throat muscles. Finally, dropping the right shoulder, stretching the neck with your head trying to touch the left shoulder.

Breathing is also a major importance, and Willie taught me how to breathe! How to bring my arms out and breathe in with an expanded chest, stretch my arms way out, stretching all the muscles round the lungs, expanding their capacity. And then breathing out like a concertina, pressing every cubic inch of air out of my lungs before doing the whole thing again. Willie gave me a lot of advice in that area and really started my awareness of simple things like that which didn't require equipment.

Although perfect eyesight is desirable it is not, in my view, a major handicap for a driver to wear spectacles. There have been several very competitive drivers over the years who did, including 1978 Indycar Champion, Tom Sneva, winner of the 1983 Indianapolis 500 at the wheel of a Bignotti/ Cotter March-Cosworth.

That's important to a person with my sort of lifestyle, whether it be as a Grand Prix driver in the past, or today, under a lot of pressure, strain and stress in the role that I play in business. A traveller cannnot be sure to find gymnastic equipment, swimming pools and so on at every location.

Later on, I discovered through the Ford Motor Company, a man named Gunther Trube. He had been working with BMW and Ford in Germany and has a training camp in St Moritz where he had been helping Ford Germany drivers get into physical shape. I think he convinced Mike Kranefuss into the belief that if you were physically fit, you could be a better racing driver. I don't think that many people in those days had clearly identified that.

I went to several of those St Moritz visits early in the season for conditioning, and it was disturbing to realise how unfit racing drivers were. Cardiovascular capacity, in particular, was terrible. Cross-country skiing, basketball, and light weight training all formed part of the daily programme, as did diet – which I will later return to.

In more recent years the man with the greatest influence on my conditioning has been a Rumanian called Radu, who had arrived in America as a refugee and now operates a very stark fifth-floor gymnasium in central Manhattan. He specialises in no-nonsense hard work to get you into shape. He is very single-minded, very determined and has an effervescent personality which somehow motivates you to take much more exercise than you would have dreamed possible.

If I was about to start motor racing seriously, I would go to Radu and have him work out a programme for me. But before I did that, I would certainly have him come to a few races just to see what a driver goes through, so that he knew the pressures – not only in the cockpit but also the kind of commitments racing brings outside the car. With a man like Radu you don't have to bounce the ball twice: he will organise an exercise programme to fit your particular lifestyle. Believe me, it really is worthwhile trying to find a fitness expert of this kind who can help an aspiring driver with a tailor-made physical training programme. This approach has particular advantages for people in high-stress situations, such as businessmen.

I think that I have a more stressful life today than I ever did when I was racing. I have to deal with those pressures without anywhere near the number of potential excuses to hand as I had when I was an active sportsman. Then, I could say that I didn't want to do anything on a Thursday because I was travelling to a Grand Prix – nor on a Monday when I was travelling back from the Grand Prix. I had cushion-time available to me. Now I am involved in endless business meetings, telephone calls late into the night, working flat-out to keep up with my commitments. And that means that the business of keeping in physical shape has become even more important to me. Radu helps me in this respect and I am sure that he, or others of his ilk, could be just as important in the lives of many other business executives.

In 1971 I had mononucleosis which is a blood disease where the white and red corpuscles don't mix. It is very common for college students who tend to burn the candle at both ends, putting in long hours of study whilst playing the games that young people play.

This is the most awful thing to get and, to this day, I don't think I ever fully recovered from it. It makes you terribly tired, a few steps away from hepatitis. I was just taking too much out of myself. In 1971 I was racing Can-Am in the United States as well as in the World Championship series. I won the World Championship and finished third in the Can-Am driving the Lola T260 for Carl Haas.

Niki Lauda (seen on the left, with McLaren team-mate Alain Prost) may appear slightly built, but his long and slender muscle structure is ideally suited to the demanding role of a sportsman. Meticulous attention to diet and a rigorous training programme, combined with tremendous self-discipline, have contributed to Lauda's success on the race track

I try to make a point of running regularly, usually each day. When I'm in London I train in Hyde Park just across the road from my base in the Grosvenor House Hotel, as these pictures show. Remember, always take the trouble to loosen up sufficiently before you get down to the serious business of running. It may be time-comsuming, but I have found it worthwhile.

I had a dismal year in 1970 with the March Formula 1, and although I had won four Formula 2 races I thought I had to let myself develop as a driver in other areas in case I was going to have another unsuccessful Grand Prix season. Although Ken had introduced his new Tyrrell car, I had made my commitment for the 1971 Can-Am season before it became clear just how good the new car might be. I was going to be taking on the might of McLaren which had dominated the Can-Am scene for years.

Bruce McLaren had died in June 1970, but his place alongside Denny Hulme in their Can-Am team had been taken by Peter Revson, so it was going to be a tough year for me. There was an awful lot of testing involved: in fact, when I hear today of some drivers complaining that they've got a lot of testing to do and 'it's not like it was in your day when it was easy . . .' I really have to smile. I think it is fair to say that in 1971 we started what was later to become the 'script' for tyre testing. Leo Mehl of Goodyear and the Tyrrell team wrote the original tyre testing book for Grand Prix racing, so to speak, and the same system is more or less used today.

On top of this, there was chassis testing for the Tyrrell and the Lola T260, and I was commuting back and forth across the Atlantic every week, interlocking Can-Am races and Grands Prix from June to October. It wasn't even that simple. The sponsorship arrangements that I had in those days were also every bit as demanding as they are for today's top drivers.

The sponsor of Haas' Can-Am Lola was L & M which was selling its racing participation in a big way to supermarkets and so on. Flying to the US on a Thursday, I was visiting shopping malls, doing speeches, press breakfasts, lunches, customer dinners at night . . . at the same time as handling a seven- or nine-hour time change, practising and racing Friday through Sunday, then getting onto an aircraft on the Sunday night, sometimes still in racing overalls. I was changing out of my thermal underwear and racing overalls in the toilet of a Boeing jetliner and getting home to Switzerland in time for breakfast on Monday morning! Then, the following weekend I would go through the same routine in Europe . . .

It was a very difficult time of my life and the pressure just got to me. I was physically unable to keep it up, and therefore I got mononucleosis. To treat that was quite a complicated issue: I really needed a complete rest which I could not allow myself then. By the time the blood tests had confirmed that I had this disorder, I was very much in the running for the World Championship. I had also led most of the Can-Am rounds and was a serious threat to McLaren.

It was a tough time. I tried to get home as often as I could, but all I would do was sleep, sleep, sleep. I was suffering from dizzy spells, I was short tempered, handling things badly. It couldn't have been a million dollars for those at home – and it wasn't for me.

Splashing through the murk towards fourth place in the 1972 Monaco Grand Prix at the wheel of my Tyrrell-Ford. It was in this race that I began to realise that I was not completely well: I had trouble co-ordinating my movements and, inexplicably, spun a couple of times during the race. This was a portent of the the stomach ulcer which would keep me away from the cockpit for six weeks at the height of that season.

101

I ended the season by winning the World Championship and, frankly, I didn't do much when I won that title. I had done the whole circuit, so to speak, when I won my first Championship in 1969. I'd received my trophy from the CSI and FIA, all the breakfasts, lunches, dinners, most of the motor shows in the world, 'state visits' to South America and so on.

It was all very good for me, educational and contributing to my knowledge of what a World Champion racing driver should have been doing. I was later to take advantage of that, particularly after I retired. But it was physically exhausting.

And like everyone in a rush, in a hurry, I was making excuses . . . I wasn't exercising, I wasn't running. I wasn't being careful about my diet. I wasn't getting enough sleep. I wasn't disciplining myself as I should have been. So in the following year, 1972, it all came home to roost because I had a duodenal ulcer that I'd been unaware of. It had been giving me some trouble, but I thought it was just part of life. But it started to bleed and it began causing very strange behaviour patterns. If I came in from the dark into a lighted room I saw stars, my equilibrium was upset and my balance affected.

One of the first races in which I realised that something was wrong was in

Back in 1973, Michael Kranefuss, chief of Ford's Cologne competitions department, organised a training schedule in Switzerland with ski coach Gunther Trube (seen with me below). I went along there with the Ford Capri touring car squad and the programme helped me considerably to get back to peak physical condition after suffering badly, first with mononucleosis and later from a stomach ulcer.

At the height of the Ford training programme with Gunther Trube: none of us realised just what poor shape we were in!

Monaco in the rain. I spun twice for no apparent reason at all. And after that race I went to Goodwood to test the McLaren Can-Am car which I'd agreed to drive that summer. I kept spinning on that day as well. I couldn't understand it. I kept making mistakes, although I didn't hit anything. When the problem was diagnosed, I had to drop out of the Can-Am programme and severely curtail my Formula 1 activities.

I went to the doctor, did all the usual tests, and it was confirmed. The ulcer was bleeding. I was then ordered off work, categorically, for six weeks. I was given three options: I could have surgery, I could stay in hospital with complete rest, or, if I was a very good boy, I could go home. So I went home. It was a wonderful summer and all I did was swim, lie in the sun, have breakfast, lie in the sun, sleep, have lunch, sleep, have a swim, have a lie in the sun, sleep . . . I was on eleven pills a day, so I was like a zombie. All I did was relax and sun myself, and it was the best six weeks of my life.

But my weight went sky-high, because at the time it was believed that the best things to eat were bread, milk, cheese, potatoes – very fattening. I ballooned to about 70 kilos. I then got back in touch with Gunther Trube. He came and lived with me. We ran every day, dieted every day, massaged every day, exercised every day, lifted light weights in a series; the whole programme lasted for six weeks.

I came back for the 1972 French Grand Prix at Clermont-Ferrand and everybody was saying 'that's the end of Stewart. He's won his two World Championships. He's gone soft. The pressure's too much for him. He's trying to earn too much money. He's going to quit now because he can't take it.' So it was very nice to come back and win the race in this very difficult year. I didn't win the title in 1972, but I won the Argentine Grand Prix – on the day my father died – then the French, Canadian and United States races. That wasn't bad.

Standing alongside the Capri RS2600 are from left to right; Hans Heyer, Kranefuss, John Fitzpatrick, Dieter Glemser, the late Gerry Birrell, Jochen Mass, JYS and Gérard Larrousse.

It was Gunther Trube's regime which really started me running much more. At the start of the 1973 season, I had made up my mind that I was never going to get ill again; I was never going to get physically or mentally out of shape. Yet I got into problems in late-spring. It was a very exhausting time of the year and by April, I was very confused. It was then that I decided I would retire. On 5 April, I told Ken Tyrrell, Walter Hayes and John Waddell of Ford that I was going to withdraw from racing. That gave me a fantastic feeling of euphoria.

The pressure had also been affecting the family. The boys were beginning to get nervous twitches, which I felt sure had their roots in what I was doing. All the racing people around us had died – Jim Clark, Jochen Rindt, Jo Bonnier, Piers Courage, Bruce McLaren. They had all been close friends and, while the boys were too young to know everything, the subconscious has a lot to do with those things. And children are very cruel to each other. I remember Paul, the elder of the two, coming home and asking his mother when I was going to die, because the boys at school had told him 'well, everybody's father dies if he's a racing driver'. It's a child's logic, if you like.

That concerned me, obviously, and these little nervous twitches were upsetting to me. I began to ask 'now what am I doing, and who am I doing it to?' That's when I made my decision to stop, irrespective of the outcome of the Championship. It gave me all the more reason to make sure that I was going to be able to fulfil my obligations that season – in real terms – so I was very fit that year.

Interestingly, I never did think I was going to win the Championship that year, or beat all the records for Grand Prix wins. But it was nice to have won Monaco for the last time.

Getting back to the topic of running. One of the elements of running for me is that one has to go through pain barriers. That's a good mental exercise. I don't think life is easy and I have a strong belief that pain has a lot to do with achievement. There are no free lunches: you only get what you pay for. If you are not prepared to put a lot of work in, then you won't get a lot out.

You need discipline in your lifestyle, because that affects anybody's achievement factor. Show me somebody who's not 'tight' in the disciplines of living, and I'll show you somebody who hasn't reached the limit of their true potential. People have a way of getting sloppy and when you get sloppy, you get careless. You forget things, there's not the same attention to detail.

It happens in all walks of life, but when you're driving racing cars the

Arnold Palmer and John McEnroe in competitive action in their respective professions. Requiring superb concentration and balance, golf and tennis are none the less not life-threatening pursuits. The ever-present potential risk to the participant is one of the most significant differences between motor racing and most other sports.

penalties can be much more severe than in most other avenues of life. I've often said an error by John McEnroe may make him mad at himself, but that error is not really a big deal. When Arnold Palmer or Tom Watson hooks into a bunker – even out of bounds – it's not life-threatening. If a racing driver, through sloppiness or lack of attention to detail, makes an error of judgement, it can have disastrous consequences. Some of the racing people who read this book live in this territory and it's one that is vastly different from most others.

That, of course, is one of the reasons why motorsport is as intoxicating and appealing as it is. The challenge of walking a tightrope of life, driving yourself to the limit of your abilities, while at the same time marrying the ultimate ability of the machine with your own, is what life is all about in a racing car. When you reach this level you feel a wonderful euphoria which, in any other sport, is rather difficult, if not impossible, to attain.

The right breakfast (above): high in fibre and roughage.

The wrong breakfast (right): too greasy, too heavy, too sweet, too much.

If you are sloppy, on the other hand, you risk paying a penalty in terms of pain and suffering far beyond almost every other sport. So I say we have to find a medium in which to tighten ourselves up, to avoid that sloppiness. That's where running helps me.

A lot of days I just don't like running, I hate the whole idea of it. In the evening I'll be tired and I may want to relax in front of the television for a while, but I'll probably go out and run. I know I'm going to have to stretch for 10 to 20 minutes, run for a minimum of 30 minutes to do myself any good at all, then stretch for another 10 minutes. And that's before having a shower or getting dressed, so it can be a two-hour schedule for me, depending on how far I run.

Two hours: that's a lot of time which I'll sometimes be under great pressure to avoid in the evening. From time to time I do avoid it. That's why I generally run in the morning. I'll be at my best and it will set me up for the rest of the day. There is no excuse to avoid it. I may have to get up early . . . but there are no free lunches!

In my opinion, you have to go through this sort of thing in order to appreciate life. You have to pay your dues. I know that if I don't run, bearing in mind the sort of lifestyle I lead, I'll get headaches, if nothing else. So I'll run for the first ten minutes, go through a discomfort period and then think 'this is worth it' and I'll be almost sorry that the run is coming to an end. But it does take time.

It's very important to get into this gradually: I think it takes about three months to become a really decent runner. A good walk, a fast walk, is a good start. Then, only after you've got your walking really going well, start running for a little while. Then walk again. Then run, then walk, then run. Over a month to eight weeks, you will find yourself running a little more and walking a little less.

Next, there is the question of diet. This does not mean simply losing weight; it involves the metabolism of the body and treating your body the right way. Take Niki Lauda: if you see him stripped to the waist you won't see an incredible body. He's almost puny. He has long muscles, they're not bulging at all. His trainer has a philosophy which builds most of his programme on diet.

I'll give you an average day's diet for me, but I always think it's nice to observe what other people have done. Niki had Willi Dungl to cook for him, prepare his meals and diet. He does that because he believes, and I believe, that the body uses up an incredible amount of energy burning up the wrong sort of food, and you could use that energy more profitably.

Think of your body as a machine. If you were to pile in normal paper through a shredder it would go through very well. If you put in a bit of aluminium foil it would be hard work for the machine to chew up. So think of that aluminium foil as the wrong food. Think how much strength that machine has to use up, think of its durability, the sharpness of the cutting edge . . . and how long it's going to last. If you put normal paper in you know the machine is going to stay in better shape for a longer time and its cutting edge is going to look good even when it's old.

So if you eat the correct food, helping all the things in your body that have to work to digest it and make it dissolve in the most efficient, most comfortable manner, the better it's going to be for you. And the strength from the proteins and the calories you're getting from that food can be put into a more purposeful effort.

There is a book with which Martina Navratilova is connected, called *Eat to Win*, which makes good reading. Jane Birbeck, who runs Bodies, an exercise and health club in London's Kings Road, introduced me to a specialist, Dick Burton, and he helped me identify that I was eating a particular packaged cereal for breakfast, thinking I was doing the right thing. He told me that it contained a lot of salt and sugar, so although it wasn't the worst thing for me, it certainly wasn't the best either.

Now I eat jumbo oats porridge for breakfast – it sounds very nationalistic – but I don't take it with salt because salt hardens the arteries, particularly for men. By eating the wrong food – tomato ketchup, french fries, all the things that we love – we can have strokes caused by narrowing arteries.

It took me a while to get into this new diet, and it is more difficult now that I no longer live the life of an athlete travelling in a team with its own special catering. In my case, staying at the grand hotels of the world, the diet is far from easy. It's not always easy getting porridge made the right way in Rio – but it can be done at Gleneagles and many other places. They'll provide it with honey and skimmed milk . . . which helps you keep cholesterol levels down. Remember, many dairy foods can be bad for you.

I tend to take a lot of soups and salads, although I'm careful about the dressing – vinegar and lemon rather than oil and vinegar (certainly not Thousand Islands or Roquefort). French vegetables are delicious to eat. Fruit isn't as good as one thinks it is because of the sugar content, but apples are fine.

Drink water rather than soft drinks. Sparkling water can be more interesting. I don't agree with the philosophy of 'you've got to have a drink . . .' I'm fortunate that my sport meant that I didn't have to prove my macho. But if I do want to have a drink, I'll take a spritzer – a mixture of white wine and sparkling mineral water. Mix to taste, whether heavy on wine or heavy on water! It gets you off the hook if you feel you're under a social obligation to drink, although I don't think that anybody should ever feel that they are under such an obligation

Alcoholism, unfortunately, is now very prevalent, even in sport. Nobody ever admits they're an alcoholic, but many have a dependency on a regular drink. People come home from the office and feel like a big strong whisky. It becomes habit-forming. Beer, in America, has become an addiction amongst the youngsters. It's like smoking a cigarette; they feel uncomfortable without something to hold in their hands.

So I've just got into the habit of not drinking. There are even some racing drivers who take a drink. But in my opinion, they would be better if they did not. I know personally that it takes time for alcohol to leave the system. Drugs are in the same category. Any mind-altering chemical generally stays in your system longer than alcohol. A doctor will tell you that, in most cases, alcohol will wash from the system in 14 hours, whereas something like marijuana will stay in the system for seven days. In many American sports cocaine, amphetamines and so forth have become a major issue. It is an illusion that they can improve performance, however. Users *think* they are performing well, but there is no question in my mind that if they were clean they would be performing better. Drugs may appear to provide a benefit in the short-term but it makes no sense at all from the long-term point of view.

From a general point of view, I know how I can perform to the best of my ability: I know that I must be hungry in every sense of the word. If I satisfy my appetite for food I am duller, more mellow, less aggressive, and I become less enthusiastic about going out and doing the job. On the other hand, if I don't eat anything for too long I'm over-edgy, over-nervous. I've got to have something in my stomach, but not very much.

It wasn't just when I was motor racing. When I was clay pigeon shooting, if I had lunch I couldn't perform to the best of my ability. It would take the edge off the lightning reaction needed to identify accurately at what height, speed and trajectory that target would be coming out of the trap, because there might well have been another target in that Olympic trench layout which had the same angle and height but a totally different speed. If you were not sharp you would over-shoot or under-shoot the target which had been put there for that specific purpose – to sort out the men from the boys.

Reaction, for me, is not necessarily how quickly I can catch a five pound note or a dollar bill dropped between my fingers. It is being able to decide clearly and positively what course of action to follow – instantly. When I had eaten I was less astute in the analysis of the messages to my brain, and was less capable of processing them and responding to them in the manner required.

Not only was this policy of remaining slightly hungry unquestionably correct for me personally, but also medically I was right. If I had an accident, the less that was in my stomach the easier it was going to be for any doctor to work on me. It's more complicated for a doctor to work on you if you've got a lot of food in your intestine. Also, it's not going to help to have your bladder full. In practical terms it's a good policy to go to the toilet, both for your bowels and your bladder, prior to the race. Now this might not seem very attractive to talk about, maybe, but practically speaking it is quite an important element of a racing driver's preparation.

Just as a full stomach made me feel slow and more satisfied, the same thing applied to sex, as far as I was concerned. I felt that if I had sex the night before or on the morning of a race it would take away that sharp edge. I wanted to be hungry and motivated. Stirling Moss said that it was not the same for him. But for me, the countdown for the race began the night before; the process of preparation. I would read myself to sleep on Harold

During the 1968 season I spent much of my time driving with this plastic support on my left wrist after I damaged the scaphoid, a tiny little bone deep within the wrist which takes a long time to heal.

112

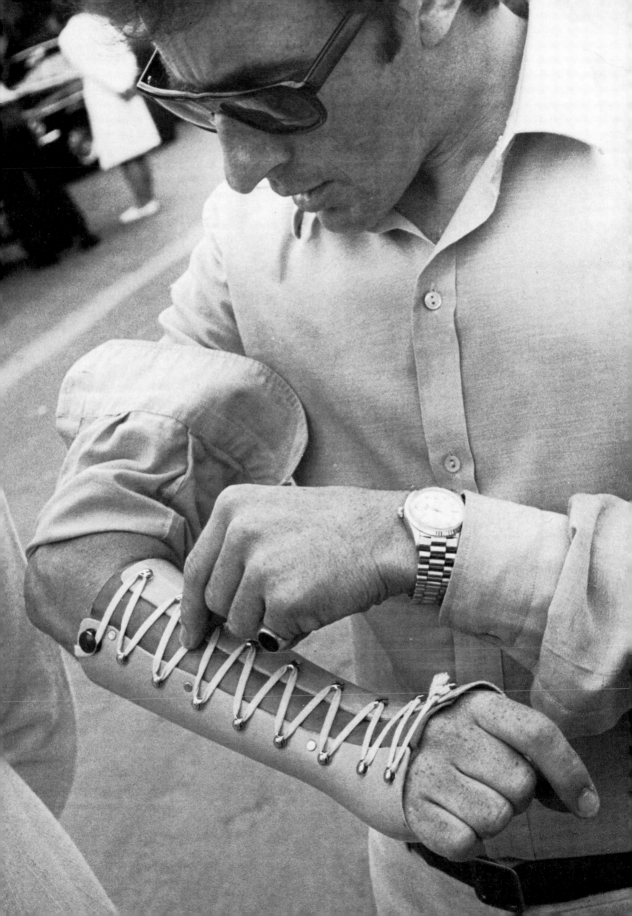

Robbins, Len Deighton, Alistair McLean ... magic carpets for me, adventures. They cleared my mind of roll bars, damper settings, the braking point for the first corner on full tanks.

However, Stirling Moss disagreed with me, and he was a great driver. Jim Clark frequently ate a big meal before the race – quite often a steak. I can recall countless times going into Geoff Murdoch's Esso Motor-home to see Jimmy consuming a great plate of steak and chips. That was the way he worked. But I knew it wasn't right for me, from my shooting experience. It might have worked well for Jimmy; but it might not have worked well for him if he'd needed emergency surgery.

I'll never forget going down to Sandown Park in Australia to drive a Lotus Cortina in 1965 and I met Roger Ward, who was then a legend in the USA and a big Indy star. And I sat there at the Southern Cross Hotel in Melbourne, and watched him eat steak with bacon, eggs, sausage and tomato ketchup, piling french fries on top and then putting strawberry jam over the whole lot! I'd never been exposed to this before and wondered whether this was some unique formula that was going to give him an incredible advantage in the race – and considered whether I should change my breakfast order of All-Bran!

For many years, much of America has been over-consuming food at a

Handicapped by that injured wrist, I struggled to sixth place with the Matra MS10 in the 1968 British Grand Prix at Brands Hatch. I had to fight an overwhelming temptation to give up and retire from the race. On my return home to Switzerland, I slept for 18 hours!

114

considerable rate. That is changing now, I think, but for sport, for racing, this question of diet must be addressed. You must consider what you have been eating and drinking and examine how it might affect you in the event of an accident. You must discipline yourself, like you discipline yourself to run; to go through the pain barriers, to know what it's like at two-thirds distance at Monaco on a hot day. Fatigue, and its effect on your rhythm and concentration, is also an aspect to consider. In almost every Grand Prix I've competed in I've felt a period of fatigue: when you get mentally tired because you're physically tired. But then you get another surge of adrenalin and you're able to overcome it. Somehow or other you survive it by mentally getting away from thinking about your aches, blisters or exhaustion. Then you get into a new rhythm and you're there.

I never managed to get a Tyrrell-entered car to handle well at Brands Hatch. In 1968 I was driving a Matra MS10 and it didn't enjoy the experience. It was, in the past, always a bumpy circuit and the car seemed to jump and dart all over the place. I was still driving with a cast on one wrist because I'd broken the scaphoid, a very small fingernail-sized bone, one of a cluster in the wrist, that gets very little blood to it and is a very slow healer. In those days it took 20 weeks to heal.

So from Monday to Friday I had my arm in a plaster cast which was then cut off for the weekend and a plastic cast would be fitted to my wrist, moulded to fit the steering wheel. It was very stressful, and I've never been so exhausted as when I finished that race. I had to be lifted from the car at the finish, even though it wasn't a particularly hot day. I got home, somehow, to Geneva, and I slept without stirring for 18 hours.

I was totally used up and it would have been very easy during that race for me to stop. Just to finish sixth and earn one Championship point wasn't much. It didn't make any difference to the outcome of the Championship, but it might have done. Had I given up I would have learned how to give up and that's a lesson I never want to learn.

It's so easy, such a comfortable route to nowhere. The devil on your shoulder says 'Oh, wouldn't it be lovely to pack it in . . . let's go home early and get into a bath.' But once you've done it, you know you can give up and then, human nature being what it is, you'll do it again.

I don't think I'm a strong person at all. But I fight hard not to be weak. Take cocaine, for example. It has become a socially acceptable activity amongst some affluent people who mix in a lifestyle that I am exposed to. I know how tired I get, weary, time-zoned, jet-lagged. From what I hear, cocaine would be a very good stimulus for me.

I've never tried it and I never want to. It has been offered to me socially even in suburbia, just like a drink or a packet of cigarettes. But what if I liked it? It could become a big problem, so I won't be trying it. The danger is that you become a slave, dependent on your pleasure. Then it ceases to be a pleasure, merely the key to the door which gives artificial means of overcoming something which your body is telling you that you shouldn't be doing. So if I'm tired, I should go to bed. My warning system, my awareness of my body, should tell me that.

Specifically, jet-lag is a problem for me. There is something about being in a pressurised aircraft fuselage for six or seven hours that does something to my body, and to almost everyone else in the world. There are exceptions, of course.

Denny Hulme, for example, would climb aboard with a copy of *Playboy* in one pocket, *Autosport* in the other, and never move from his seat for the entire journey. He would eat everything put in front of him, be as happy as a lark and step off the other end as if he'd just got off the number nine bus!

I am not so lucky. Jet-lag entirely disturbs my sleeping and eating patterns, as well as disrupting all my bodily functions. Each aspect of my person is in a strange and disorderly state. Therefore, when I travel, I have to live by certain rules. I cannot drink alcohol of any kind on a plane, unless I am on a night flight when I sometimes give myself the privilege of a glass of champagne to help me sleep. Otherwise I want still, bottled water. I hardly eat at all. Occasionally I have vegetarian meals, but generally I eat as little as possible. When I get out at the other end, I sometimes go for a long walk or a gentle run – not too hard, but just enough to get my body moving again. Then a nice hot bath before I go to bed will help me recover.

Funnily enough, I always find that it is the third night of my stay that I sleep the least when I have been subjected to a time change of more than seven hours. But I'm very lucky to be able to catnap for ten to fifteen minutes and that's enough to recharge my batteries. When it comes to business meetings, my advice is that you try to complete the meeting in the morning before lunch has been served. Get people when they are fresh, before a heavy lunch has made them either over-boisterous or indecisive.

Despite this, I think I'm fairly astute as far as understanding my body messages. I know when my blood pressure is up, when I'm under stress, when my pulse rate is high. I go every year to the Mayo Clinic in Rochester, Minnesota, which is probably the best diagnostic clinic in the world. I go there because I think it's the best. It is money well spent, despite the expense and inconvenience. I have confidence in the place and believe that regular medical check-ups are really worthwhile.

I'll never forget Gunnar Nilsson, who contracted cancer at 28 years old. He went to a couple of doctors who perhaps didn't treat him as astutely as they should have done. He was getting dizzy, not feeling at all well. Eventually, Frank Faulkner, a professor of paediatrics who has been a friend of the motor racing community for many years, got involved. After hearing the symptoms on the telephone, Frank sent him to a colleague at Charing Cross hospital, London, who specialised in what Frank feared it might be: cancer.

Gunnar was admitted at eleven o'clock – and they were operating on him at two in the afternoon. In eleven months he was dead. Maybe, if he had noticed those tell-tale warnings, he could have been operated on in time. By the time Charing Cross Hospital started treating Gunnar, the cancer, which had originally started low in his body, had spread to his kidneys, his stomach, his lungs, his heart and his brain. From being a wonderful physical specimen he was reduced to a wreck of human frailty in eleven months.

That is an extreme example, I know. Nevertheless, whether it be the start of a duodenal ulcer or something more minor, early treatment may help to avoid a more serious problem later on.

Chapter 4
The High Speed Technique

There is, I think, an element of confusion about the way in which competition drivers and high-performance drivers handle and 'communicate' with their cars at high speeds in a circuit environment. A common belief exists that the racing driver's technique is all arms and elbows; in fact one particular great Australian philosopher/racing driver, Frank Gardner, once said that when a racing driver was looking spectacular he resembled a paper-hanger in a thunderstorm: all arms and elbows, trying to get the paste and the paper on the walls at the same time with the wind whistling through open windows! But it shouldn't be like that.

Good racing drivers are smooth, clean and unspectacular. Those drivers are the ones that people notice least on the track, although they tend to emerge as the quickest because they are not wasting their energy slipping and sliding all over the place. They concentrate more acutely on following a clean line through a corner, applying their energies to getting the car round with the least friction and rolling resistance. If you get a car sideways, its tyres are scrubbing against the road surface, you're slowing yourself down. You have to apply more throttle. When you apply more throttle, you're using more fuel. As a Scotsman, that might have been the main reason why I always used little throttle!

So it is a question of being able to drive economically: not merely from the point of view of the car, but also from the human physical standpoint. If you are driving long races it can become physically very tiring. If you drive at ten-tenths, at the absolute limit of yourself and your car for the whole race, you simply would not be able to sustain the effort for a three-, six- or twenty-four-hour race. Therefore you have to be able to conserve not only your car, your fuel, your tyres, your suspension, your engine and your gearbox, but also yourself.

My own views on how a high-performance car, or any car, should be driven should be seen in conjunction with the accompanying sketches. The essence of the whole philosophy is *finesse*. You should not have a situation where a driver roars away from traffic lights and the passenger's head bangs against the headrest, or loose papers fly off the parcel shelf. Likewise, when you brake, there should be no question of suddenly launching the occupants against their seat belts. It should be a gentle progression of acceleration and deceleration, exactly the same on the road as on the race track, because competition and road cars are designed on similar principles.

Let us consider Figure 1, with the car in its static condition. When an engineer designs a car, he considers wheel movement: being able to get clear, unimpeded suspension movement up and down. This allows the car to

This car is sliding untidily, dissipating its energy in an ineffective and wasteful fashion. The steering will feel heavy and sluggish as the overtaxed outside front tyre is distorted and scrubbed against the road surface.

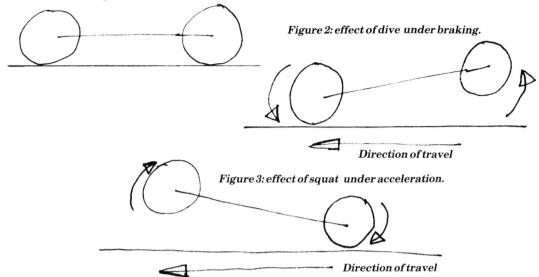

Figure 1: car in static configuration.

Figure 2: effect of dive under braking.

Direction of travel

Figure 3: effect of squat under acceleration.

Direction of travel

ride comfortably over bumps and undulations, allowing the suspension system to accommodate potholes, bumps and compressions in every way possible. Similarly, when going round a corner the car wants to roll, so the suspension movement has to allow for that. When a racing car arrives at a corner – perhaps reaching 180 to 200 mph for a contemporary Formula 1 car – there are several crucial aspects to consider.

You must recognise the braking distance, the entry point to the corner, the apex and the exit point. When you go into this at 180 mph there is no question of immediately taking your foot right off the throttle in one sudden movement. Of course you will need to move your foot from the throttle, but the importance lies in *how* you do this. If you take it off suddenly (and you can encounter the feeling if you back off quickly at 30 mph in second or third gear in your road car) you will feel the car begin to nose down the moment you lift your foot. This is because the forward motion has been sharply reduced, so the general weight distribution of the car will shift towards the front. This is fairly straightforward when you think about it. Similarly, if you hit the brake pedal, then the nose of the car will immediately dive, compressing the front suspension. The nose goes down and the tail comes up (see Figure 2).

If we think of that in exaggerated terms you find the front end goes right down and the rear comes right up in quite dramatic fashion. If this was a racing car or a rally car (which have far less suspension movement than road cars), the suspension can 'bottom out' and hit the bump rubbers, which stop the car hitting the road when the suspension compresses to the limit of its travel. Beyond that there is no more suspension movement.

If, during that time, you hit any bumps on the road surface, there is no suspension movement left to accommodate them, so the car 'patters' over those bumps. Should the driver be trying to turn the car into a corner when that happens, the car will patter across the road instead of taking the desired line of the corner, probably introducing the phenomenon called understeer, or 'push' as it is termed in America.

Simultaneously, the rear end will be reacting. The moment you attempt to turn into the corner the rear wheels are light on the ground because the tyres are not getting the benefit of a full footprint on the road surface. The rear suspension is 'on droop', which means it is not pressing the tyres down firmly on the road. So the car's back end will kick out, causing oversteer. If this is not corrected the car will simply spin off the track (unless you apply opposite lock – by steering into the skid).

You can of course apply a lot of power in a racing car. Current turbocharged Grand Prix racing cars are producing anything from 750 bhp to 1100 bhp. So you've got a lot of stick there and you can control that slide to a considerable degree. But when you're controlling it on the throttle you are burning rubber, using fuel, putting tyre temperatures up. Keeping tyre temperatures within the correct range is absolutely essential and fundamental to the performance of the car for the entire duration of the race.

As you steer into the corner, that outside front suspension is going through all sorts of acrobatics. The nose is down, you turn in and understeer develops. Then suddenly the rear end breaks away and you apply the power. Then the opposite happens. When 750 bhp is applied through the rear wheels, we now have power and weight transfer from front to rear. Applying the power pulls the rear end down, as in Figure 3.

This is a new attitude, then: the back end is down and the front end is up. The rear suspension is now fully compressed and is giving us the same problem, because the bumps cannot be accommodated. The rear end is pattering out, inducing more oversteer, but that oversteer cannot be controlled by applying power onto the road nearly as well because there's no suspension to accommodate it. So when it hits those corrugations, it sets up a vibration in the transmission, and if we are in second or third gear with 750 bhp on tap you can imagine what is happening to the gearbox, couplings, suspension and, in fact, to the entire car. The vibration is giving the car hell . . . and storing up potential mechanical problems, because racing cars have necessarily to be light to be competitive and, as a consequence, tend to be quite fragile.

The speed at the end of a straight is precisely determined by the speed at which we come out of the previous corner onto that straight. We are talking, in racing terms, of margins of one or two hundred engine revs per minute. We might be patting ourselves on the back for negotiating that corner very well, gaining those two hundred revs on the exit; if we have misjudged it and don't get the exit right it means that we have to back off a bit, perhaps running over the kerb on the outside of the corner and needing to back off the throttle just a wee bit. In doing so, we will lose that fraction of forward motion. That means we're going to reduce our maximum possible speed down the next straight – and it might be the only opportunity to pass the car in front in the entire lap. What's more, if we're the one who makes the error, then the driver behind is probably going to pass into the braking area for the next corner because he's had a run at us all the way down that straight.

The process of bringing the rear end down to squat by attacking the throttle too aggressively will therefore bring up the front end too much. Because the front end is in the air you can't steer it as precisely. You can't position it correctly, you can't hit your apex accurately, therefore you can't exit as quickly, all because the attitude of the car doesn't allow the front tyres to give you the grip that it would ideally produce.

So what's the way out of all this? Essentially, you must drive smoothly, handling the car with finesse. When you come into the corner you should release the throttle gently, to the point where you are not really aware of the car slowing down, then brake progressively, very gently to begin with.

Similarly, bring your foot off the brake pedal gently and progressively. The whole sequence should be one gentle, sensitive, flowing movement. You want the nose of the car to come up gently and undramatically. You want to get the car off its bump rubbers before you turn into the corner, so that there is some suspension movement remaining to accommodate the roll which will follow.

I must make it clear that this technique is not something which I employed consciously throughout my racing career, it was something which took me a great many years to understand and execute. It was not until the end of 1968 that I was fully able to think through the process and began applying that process to the actual physical business of driving. For a long time I drove by the seat of my pants, using a God-given gift.

Some young drivers may find this concept difficult to grasp. People will say, 'it's all too much of a rush, you can't do all those things smoothly, gently and slowly at the sort of speeds we are doing, there just is not enough time!' But believe me, it can work. It takes years to develop, but suddenly things go into slow motion in your mind, your vision, your synchronisation, and you find yourself in a position to achieve it.

In the mid-1970s, we created something which enabled me to demonstrate this principle to people who had perhaps never had the opportunity of driving on a race circuit or test track. This was 'Formula Finesse', a very simple test involving a shallow 'salad bowl' attached to the bonnet of a road car containing a ball. We mapped out a route in and out of a sequence of pylons in a figure of eight and the object was to drive through

The Sierra XR 4x4 is cornering quickly, as evidenced by the degree of roll it has assumed, but it is doing so in a totally neutral manner with its front tyres addressing the road surface in the manner intended by the tyre manufacturer. In these circumstances the steering will feel pleasantly light, though without any trace of vagueness in its response

In a road racing car understeer is both time-wasting and tiring. This photograph of my BRM V8 on its way to second place behind Jim Clark's Lotus in the 1965 French Grand Prix at Clermont-Ferrand indicates how badly the front tyres were wearing owing to an understeer problem. Below, wrestling the March 701 round Clubhouse corner at Kyalami during the 1970 South African Grand Prix provides another example of understeer. In fact, this car was an unpredictable handful which was tiring to drive and could never be tuned into any semblance of consistently competitive form. The Sierra photographed here at Donington is going through similar contortions.

while keeping the ball in the dish. It was all first and second gear stuff. Very easy, you might think, but not as simple as it appears at first glance.

The idea was to drive round very gently. It provided an excellent and uncomplicated way of demonstrating just what happened when you braked or accelerated or corrected violently – the ball flew out of the dish. It was a very straightforward example of the philosophy I have explained in connection with smoothness under braking and turn-in to corners. What's more, you could have visual proof when doing it wrong. The Formula Finesse concept enabled one to see the point quite graphically at low speeds in a confined environment.

Let's turn our attention now to sliding. The main issue to consider when a car starts sliding is whether it is sliding in the right attitude. The attitude in which the car slides has everything to do with the exit speed of the vehicle, particularly addressing the next straight stretch of road following the corner we are examining.

As you turn into the corner you have to set up the car in such a way, anticipating the amount of slip it will develop, so that the car still brushes the apex of the corner at exactly the point you originally intended it to. Remember, of course, that it is the exit point which is the most important part of any corner, a fact which many people regularly overlook. If you hit too early an apex, you then hit too early an exit, forcing you to reduce power and arrest the slide to readdress the angle of the vehicle to where the corner actually finishes.

If that corner is finishing too early for the car's attitude, it means you have to reduce the forward momentum of the car or you might run out of the road, or even kiss the wall (maybe *too* firmly!) in a street circuit.

Adopting a comfortable and effective driving position, not too far away from the steering wheel, is an important prerequisite of efficient car control. In this sequence of pictures I am turning the steering wheel progressively as the car approaches the apex of the corner, but the position of my hand on the steering wheel remains the same. Although there are some experts, including the police, who prefer passing the wheel through the hands when negotiating the corner, I believe that my method is the right one. Note the angle of my arms at the elbow when I am holding the steering wheel in a straight line: I am close enough to the wheel to turn it as far as I may need without ever having to stretch too far.

Under braking the car will develop a nose-down attitude ('dive') when the weight distribution moves forwards and the rear wheels are light — as seen in Figure 2 and the accompanying photograph of my BRM 2-litre braking hard during the 1967 French Grand Prix at Le Mans. Conversely, under acceleration the rear of the car goes down on its suspension ('squat') and the nose tends to come up. This is illustrated in Figure 3 and in the view of Graham Hill's Lotus 49. Modern cars do not demonstrate these qualities to such a visually obvious extent but minimising the unsettling effect on a car's handling through a corner caused by these two phenomena is no less crucial. I regularly use straightforward sketches in blackboard sessions to illustrate these characteristics in an uncomplicated manner.

The Formula Finesse exercise is a simple way to make the point that smooth driving pays off. One of these drivers has successfully mastered the knack and the ball remains in the dish on the bonnet of the Sierra; the other driver's less smooth technique has caused the ball to jump out of the dish and emphasises to him the need to polish up his style.

Thinking back to the days when the term 'four-wheel drift' was coined, recalls a wonderful photograph of Fangio driving a supercharged Alfa Romeo 158 back in the early 1950s. He had this car with all its skinny tyres sliding, yet all those tyres were pointing straight ahead, even if the cambers looked rather strange. The wheels were not showing even a trace of understeer or oversteer, and that is the way the car must be driven if you are reaching the ultimate limit of adhesion. But there's no point in getting things looking right for the trackside photographers if the car does not strike the apex at exactly the right point to guarantee that the slide's momentum finishes precisely at the end of the corner, thus enabling all the power to be applied cleanly, without the car actually feeling that it has reached the end of the corner.

To repeat: you should never feel the end of the corner, because you need to accelerate through that turn in truly progressive style. You should never feel any lateral G-forces as you enter the next straight. They should have been progressively absorbed in the corner itself, leaving the car to propel itself down the following straight utilising its maximum power potential. The exit point of a corner is of paramount importance.

Tight hairpins, of course, pose some very specific problems, both in terms of car control and self-control on the part of the driver. I have to say at this point that I never really considered myself fast through tight corners. I never thought, for example, that I got Druids bend at Brands Hatch really right, yet on paper it was the slowest and simplest corner on the whole circuit.

I don't like the idea of deliberately kicking the rear end out as part of a driver's technique for dealing with a tight hairpin. I don't think it should be part of a driver's repertoire: once learned, the technique will inevitably be abused. I'm not saying that it shouldn't happen, but it should be by accident rather than design.

There are times when a car is understeering so badly into a tight hairpin that it is necessary to introduce an element of oversteer in order to counter the problem. This quite frequently happens on a track with a lot of fast corners which you have accommodated with very small amounts of front downforce. You can have a lot of frontal downforce on a quick circuit because the car pivots round the front end in an alarmingly over-responsive fashion. Of course, when you arrive at a slow corner with the car in this configuration, there is perhaps inadequate downforce at speeds below, say, 100 mph.

Suddenly, the car will not have the same amount of 'bite' that it has displayed on other sections of the circuit. Under those circumstances, the driver may have to kick the tail out a bit in order to hit the correct apex. But don't get the car so far into an oversteering stance that you must start controlling it all with the throttle. If you should hit a patch of oil and water in this sort of situation you can suddenly find yourself caught out. Don't get into a position which may be entertaining the spectators, but only a degree or so away from a spin. Remember, one spin can destroy a whole race.

Imagine now that you've run wide and you are on the marbles. The biggest issue at this point is to avoid spinning and damaging the car.

Sometimes it might seem easy to run over the kerb, onto the grass, keep your foot on the throttle and drive through the drama. But you have to consider and calculate what sort of surface you might be about to cross. Will the car accommodate that terrain? Will the car dig in and, possibly, even turn over? This could not only end your day and your race, but conceivably your life as well, so the watchword must be to take the line of least resistance from the car's point of view.

So try and get that slide angle off. If you are running short of road, you might be able to rescue the situation by going over the kerb – as long as you know what is beyond. In that connection, there is still the opportunity for a young racing driver to walk the race track and see what awaits on the outside of each corner exit. If you don't want to be seen walking the track there may be a way of driving round slowly in a road car before the meeting begins. I see Ayrton Senna doing this regularly, possibly more often than any other driver. Follow his example: go and have a look.

It may be difficult at some circuits, but if you go to the Clerk of the Course sufficiently early in the weekend, and explain why you want to do it, he's going to be more impressed with you than he will be if you go flying off the track because of your lack of knowledge. Remember, detailed preparation is the key to success in all professional activities, whether business or sport.

However, let's assume that, despite all these precautions and considerations, you have lost it and the car has spun. First of all, have a good look round. There are one or two drivers who become completely disorientated the moment they spin: in fact, I have even known one driver who resumed lapping *against* the direction of traffic following a spin!

Take stock of the situation. Where possible, keep your engine running. Whether you are driving a touring car or a single-seater, when high-performance engines stop, they are usually very hot. It is sometimes very difficult indeed to restart hot competition engines. You frequently encounter fuel vapourisation, particularly with a turbocharged engine, and this can aggravate the problem.

In these situations, remember the adage 'when in doubt, both feet out'. That means the brake and the clutch pedal. If you dip the clutch, the engine may keep running. Of those people reading this book, there will be just one per cent able to accommodate the technique of blipping the throttle with the side of their right foot as they are, simultaneously, throwing out both the clutch and the brake pedals. I failed to do it on some occasions, yet felt very pleased with myself when I managed to do it on others. If you can't keep the engine running but have time to select a gear while the wayward car is still moving you may be able to 'bump start' the car again, which is the next best thing to keeping the engine running in the first place. Once you've spun, weigh up where you have come to rest on the road. Pay attention to the flag marshals because they are your only source of information. It may be a blind corner and you won't know who is coming round next. So don't move until signalled to do so by the marshals. Race marshalling, worldwide, is of an ever-improving standard so, in most cases, the balance of your judgement should fall in their favour.

If you are not going to be able to turn round within the width of the circuit with the steering lock you have available, you may be able to spin the rear wheels and flick the car round in its own length. But even the most experienced drivers can get caught out by this technique. For example, Alain Prost at the 1985 German Grand Prix at the Nürburgring had to go round twice because he made a big error recovering from a spin. Similarly, some people think that they can drive away over the grass run-off area with

Improvisation is a necessary part of the repertoire of a competition driver, as this shot of my BRM H16 leaping a crest at the original 14-mile Nürburgring Nordschleif indicates only too well. Although I believe the circuit represented an unrealistic and unacceptable risk, it did sharpen one's sense of anticipation and ability to read signs of impending difficulties. This BRM was a particularly difficult car to drive as it seemed to have its own limited performance plateau beyond which it could not be taken by an individual's driving ability.

impunity. But the grass is not always billiard-table smooth and can do a lot
of damage to your car. You may pick up dangerous debris on the tyres or
destroy the aerodynamic attachments at the front end. You are driving a
specialist racing car, not a tank designed to go off across country!

Another important consideration is giving yourself time to settle down
again after such an incident. I've never known a driver who, after making a
mistake, will be able to go into the next four or five corners as if nothing had
happened. They are always uncomfortable, always need to settle their
emotions down, and that's not an easy thing to do. If you find a driver in that
condition, that is the time to take advantage of him. But be careful – he may
well do something unpredictable! Nevertheless, you know he is flustered, so
take that opportunity to put him under even more pressure. Don't
immediately dive in at what seems the first opportunity. Give him a little
space, but keep the pressure up. This is an important lesson in racecraft;
not many people think clearly under high-pressure conditions like that,
believe me.

On the subject of gear changing techniques, I have always believed that
you should take as little out of the car's transmission as possible. That
obviously means gentle, sympathetic changes when going up through the
gears, but also by using the brakes to their maximum when slowing down,

often missing gears while changing down through the box. Many people think that racing drivers go all the way down through the gears in a six-speed box like a machine gun. But that means you're taking on a juggling act: steering, operating the pedals, blipping the throttle and using the gear lever like a madman.

I always chose to change down by jumping through gears. I didn't in the early part of my career, but as I was able to develop more controlled pace into my driving I began changing from fifth to third to first or, in a six-speed box, from sixth to fourth to second. That applies to wet or dry conditions, although you need to be careful how you do it in the wet, perhaps eliminating all the downchanges, using the brakes to knock off your speed, and then finally slipping from sixth to first gear right at the end. Remember, you are not going to stop any faster by using the transmission. Brakes are made to stop a car, gears are primarily for acceleration. Deceleration was not part of the gearbox's original purpose; don't abuse it.

On the way up through the box you can also jump gears to beneficial effect, although the concept may sound rather strange. Coming out of Druids at Brands Hatch I would go directly from second to fourth gear. I

The development of aerodynamic devices has brought another dimension to chassis tuning and my career spanned the era of experimentation with their early manifestations. My Tyrrell-Matra MS80 reveals how little we understood about the business of detailed aerodynamics in 1969. Note particularly that the absence of side plates on the end of the wings allowed airflow to peel untidily off the side. The side plates would have prevented this aerodynamic 'spill'.

was going downhill and I could not apply all the power in any case, because I would have to come off the throttle in third gear for Bottom Bend. Therefore, I would change slowly from second to fourth: it meant that the car would not accelerate so quickly in fourth gear, but it would be more settled in its attitude as I went through Bottom Bend and on that section of the track nobody could pass me anyway. This technique may have relatively few applications but there are *some* and it is worth bearing this in mind because the net result is to take less out of the car mechanically.

The other time I would change up early was on an undulating circuit, like the old Nürburgring or the original 'long' Oulton Park. Although I would be changing slightly before maximum revs, I might be going downhill: it was easier on the car. At the Nürburgring, I used to change up a gear when the car was in the air over the bumps.

A word about the 'heel and toe' technique for keeping the engine revving while you are shifting down gear. Heel-and-toeing never existed in the sense its name suggested: in real terms one just rolled the side of one's right foot off the brake pedal and blipped the throttle momentarily as required. Perhaps, way back in history, the initiator of this technique may have had a pedal configuration which literally required him to employ this technique, but the practical reality of the concept today simply involves the side of the foot.

In order to be as easy on the car as possible, make it a general rule to try to run one gear higher than you initially think necessary. This also gives you more scope for improvement. If you are accelerating out of a corner in fourth gear, you may have a 500 rpm bank in which to improve the performance of that car before you change up. If you execute the corner outstandingly well, you might only have a 200 rpm margin through which to improve. But had you been in a higher gear there might have been 1000 rpm left: the car exits faster and receives less wear and tear. So, when you are able to change your gear ratios always try to select one ratio higher than you imagine you will need. If you have to back off the throttle for any reason when the engine is high in its rev range, the power transfer will be less marked if you are in a higher gear. The car will therefore be significantly less nervous to drive.

When you actually start a race I believe that you should drive the first lap as quickly as you possibly can. In fact, few drivers are capable of just 'flicking a switch' and running fast from the outset. The greatest personal advantage I ever had in professional racing was an ability to switch on and perform as well on my first lap as I did mid-way through the race, or on the last lap. Most of my victories were achieved by breaking the opposition early on. Most people I raced against had an unsettling first five laps or so: they were uptight, nervous and generally not settled in as well as they would be later on.

In 1971 French Grand Prix, my Tyrrell shared the front row with the Ferrari flat-12s of Jacky Ickx and Clay Regazzoni. If those Ferraris had been with me after five laps then they would have won the race. I couldn't have stayed with them in a straight line and, for certain, they would have slipstreamed past me on that long back straight.

So the first lap is terribly important – but the second lap is even more important. On the second lap you don't know who has dropped what: you can find patches of water, oil or even fuel. For example, Mike Parkes crashed his Ferrari on the second lap of the 1967 Belgian Grand Prix at Spa-Francorchamps when he hit oil dropped by my BRM H16, although I didn't know it at the time.

Oversteer can be time-wasting as well, although it is less frustrating than understeer. Denny Hulme's Brabham-Repco V8 during the 1967 French Grand Prix at Le Mans displays a touch of oversteer but nothing likely to cause too much trouble – this is merely a reflection of driver preference rather than any indication of an inherent handling imbalance.

135

Heavy braking

KYALAMI – SUNSET

*Sunset should be entered a little to the left of the centre of the road.
The line follows the contour of the corner rather than 'diamonding'
the bend which might seem the ideal line. As in most corners, try a
higher gear than appears right for the bend because this will
produce more engine revs and thereby increase cornering speed.
If a lower gear is used in such a long corner it's likely that the
engine will 'run out of breath' too early to allow a good fast exit.
Also, the car will be less affected by engine braking on the entry to
the corner. Changing down too low makes the car nervous and
over-responsive to the throttle; a higher gear makes the car more
docile. Most drivers change gear too often. Braking for Sunset is a
very gentle process and the car should be disturbed as little as
possible. The throttle application should be a gentle and
progressive pressure – not on and off throughout the corner as this
will badly upset the car.*

The following comments and observations about the way in which I tackled specific corners on certain circuits are of a general nature based on my own experiences, mainly in Ford-Cosworth V8-powered Formula 1 cars. Gearchange points may differ in cars from other categories, but these remarks will provide a blueprint for handling most types of corner likely to be encountered.

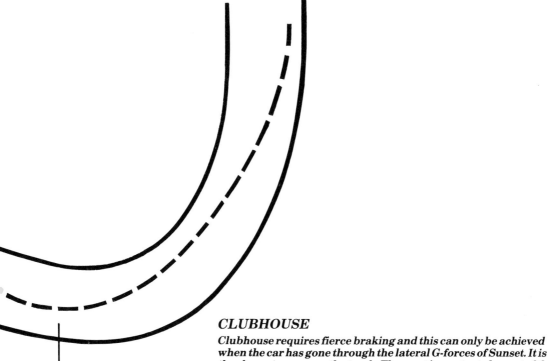

Bring nose
up (let brakes off)
before turning
into Clubhouse

CLUBHOUSE

Clubhouse requires fierce braking and this can only be achieved when the car has gone through the lateral G-forces of Sunset. It is the slowest corner on the track. The most important element of the braking distance is not when the brakes are applied but when and how they are released! The driver must allow the nose of the car to come up (by taking the brakes off gently) before turning the car into the left-hand corner. Because it is a relatively slow corner, a fair amount of exuberance is generally exercised at Clubhouse and a lot of oversteer is in evidence. On many occasions this is because drivers have not allowed the car to come off the bump rubbers at the front after braking heavily before turning into the corner. The suspension therefore has nothing left to accommodate the roll and the car will not turn in as it should, which can result in the apex being missed. The driver is left with no option but to induce oversteer to avoid running out of road on the exit. More liberties are taken in slow corners than in fast ones for obvious reasons. However, when oversteer is induced unnecessarily, tyre temperatures are forced up, dramatically affecting the car's handling over a full race distance.

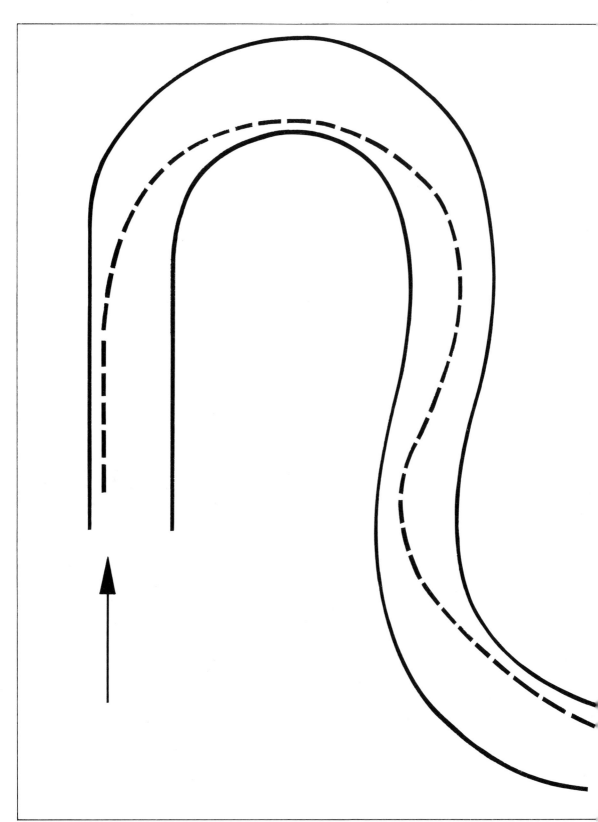

BRANDS HATCH – DRUIDS/ GRAHAM HILL BEND

Fierce braking is the order of the day at Druids but, again, the brakes should be taken off gently and progressively. Some people believe that a driver should brake into a corner and turn in whilst still on the brakes. I do not agree with this. You will end up 'dirt tracking' a lot of corners, which will, in the long term, take a lot out of the car, brakes and driver. Get most of your braking done before turning into Druids and you will retain far more control. If you miss the apex a lot of time and road is needed to correct the error, affecting your exit and the entry to the next corner, which is an extremely important one as it leads to a fast part of the circuit. A variety of lines are used at Druids so it is really a very 'personal' bend. The exit, however, is very important. Because of the steep downhill descent, it is possible, in most cars, to change straight from second to fourth gear before committing the car to Graham Hill bend. By doing this the car will be more docile and the driver is left free for this relatively short piece of track. Changing from second to third and then fourth gear in fierce acceleration while the car's weight distribution moves from left to right can be quite a juggling act. Every time there is a gear change the weight is transferred from front to rear on acceleration, so the fewer gear changes the better on this particular section of the track. There is a tendency to hit an early apex at Graham Hill bend and this will usually cost you time. What normally occurs is that you run out of road on the exit and have to reduce power to avoid running onto the grass. This is also a corner where understeer can show up, so placing the car to hit the correct apex is extremely important. It's for this reason that the driver should leave Druids cleanly, with as little fuss and distraction as possible so that plenty of time and attention can be devoted to Graham Hill bend. There is much more time to be lost or gained there.

MONTE CARLO – MASSENET / CASINO SQUARE

Entering the long left-hand bend in the centre of the road, The car becomes very light as it goes over the crest of the hill. You drive through the corner by staying fairly close to the kerb all the way round while still avoiding the drainage grills and rain gutter. The apex is hit very late and you should try to go through the left-hander in as high a gear as possible. This is a far faster corner than it appears and few people get it right.

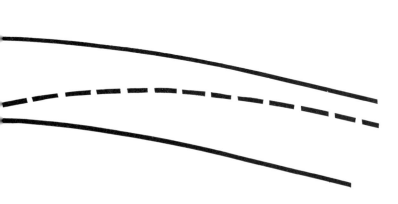

On the descent from Casino Square do not use all the road on the left side of the right-hander. There are quite a few bumps and undulations and the car needs space, just in case it darts to the left or the oversteer increases. As a general rule, do not use all the road at Monaco – sooner or later you will hit a barrier. There is a great temptation to over-drive Monaco but this should be avoided. I have found quite often that a slower driving style gives me a faster time in the end. This is a track that needs finesse in one's approach.

the end of the left-hander the car should be as settled as possible
accommodate the change of attitude from left to right. Oversteer
definite advantage here; there is too much to do in too short a
e. The highest gear possible should be chosen because
mediately beyond the apex of the right-hander there is a
crest, which tends to make the car light at the rear thus
ucing oversteer. A higher gear ratio will reduce the likelihood
his and allow the driver more time.

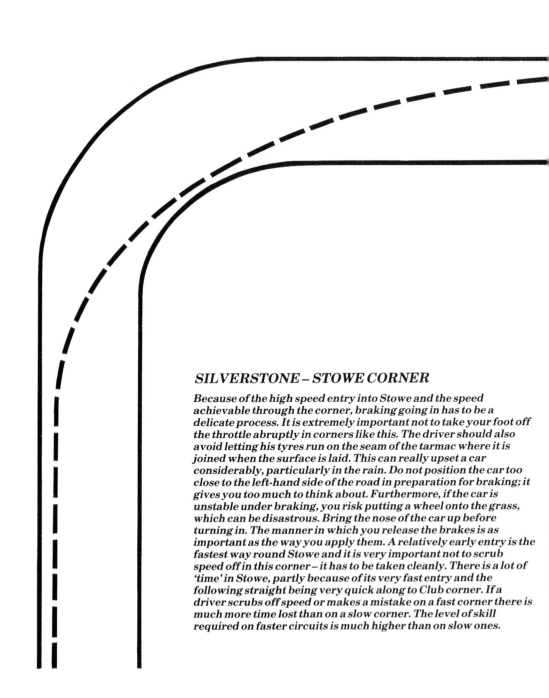

SILVERSTONE – STOWE CORNER

*Because of the high speed entry into Stowe and the speed
achievable through the corner, braking going in has to be a
delicate process. It is extremely important not to take your foot off
the throttle abruptly in corners like this. The driver should also
avoid letting his tyres run on the seam of the tarmac where it is
joined when the surface is laid. This can really upset a car
considerably, particularly in the rain. Do not position the car too
close to the left-hand side of the road in preparation for braking; it
gives you too much to think about. Furthermore, if the car is
unstable under braking, you risk putting a wheel onto the grass,
which can be disastrous. Bring the nose of the car up before
turning in. The manner in which you release the brakes is as
important as the way you apply them. A relatively early entry is the
fastest way round Stowe and it is very important not to scrub
speed off in this corner – it has to be taken cleanly. There is a lot of
'time' in Stowe, partly because of its very fast entry and the
following straight being very quick along to Club corner. If a
driver scrubs off speed or makes a mistake on a fast corner there is
much more time lost than on a slow corner. The level of skill
required on faster circuits is much higher than on slow ones.*

It's best to run the first lap as quickly as you can, then treat the second lap with great caution, before building up to your ultimate limit from the third lap onwards.

Let's look now at driving technique in a road car, examining some of the prerequisites of being able to perform in an effective, efficient and economical style. The first and most important element is to be in the correct driving position. You should be able to grip the top of the steering wheel with a clenched fist and a bent arm without having to move your shoulders from the back of the seat rest. In an emergency, when you may have to rush for something, it is very important to be able to reach easily without having to stretch or without being congested by sitting too close to the steering wheel. Most people think racing drivers sit far away from the steering wheel with their arms straight. This is not true.

Outside Formula 1, driving techniques have to be adapted slightly depending on what sort of car one is driving, but the essential requirements remain unchanged. I am seen here in a Ford Capri RS at Paul Ricard during 1973, sharing with François Cevert.

Try lifting a weight with your arms straight out in front of you – you can't do it. You *can* do it with bent arms. The same principle applies in a car. Any effort should be applied through slightly bent arms.

I always like to draw the analogy that motoring quickly is rather like being on the deck of a yacht, using your legs to absorb the motion of the vessel. If you were on the deck of a yacht in a rough sea, you wouldn't be standing with your feet and legs together. If your legs are slightly apart, knees flexing, your feet splayed; with one foot slightly ahead of the other, you could handle amost any sea! The position of your feet in the footwell of a road or racing car is also very similar. The same thing applies to your head which has got to stay with the motion. If you take your head off the stock of a gun your eye no longer goes down the barrel sighting or the bead of that gun. To shoot accurately your head must stay on the stock until you have pulled the trigger. In a car, if you're going to the right, cock your head very slightly in that direction. Nothing too dramatic, of course, just try to keep your body all together. There's no need to wave your head round in the wind.

Hand positions on the steering wheel at 'ten-to-two' – that's about the best position. Rather than shuffling the wheel through my hands, I cross my arms, although if I'm going into a hairpin corner I might slightly reposition my hands on the rim. During a race I tended always to keep the same place, thumb over the spoke, at the ten-to-two position.

When you start off, whether it be in a road or a racing car, there should be no jerky power take-up as you drop the clutch. If there is, you will hear the universal couplings in the transmission being unnecessarily exercised. Even if we are driving away quickly from a standing start, we should be able to do it quickly without even feeling the gearchanges.

If you go into a corner, bear in mind what I have been saying about the application of throttle and brakes. I've demonstrated it many times. And when you come out of the corner you should allow the car to run as wide as you can: let it run free, like a horseman giving a horse its head, or a yacht whose keel is cutting cleanly through the water, rather than attacking the water abrasively with side-slip. You should never actually be able to feel where the corner ends or the next straight begins.

Similarly, you should never feel the car coming to a stop. When you apply the brakes gently, you should be able to go down through the gearbox and come smoothly to a halt. There should be no dipping of the front end or disturbing the occupants. So whether you're a good chauffeur or a good racing driver, it's exactly the same technique.

Most people try to steer more and more into the corner when they experience the first indications of understeer, but in fact they are increasing the problem because the tyres were never designed to attack the road at an extreme angle. The tyres were designed to face the road with their full profile, not with the sidewall. All that happens in this situation is that the tyres are being turned even more against their ideal path. In other words, they are showing more of the sidewall to the up-coming road surface rather than the tread. So they are increasing the understeer rather than decreasing it.

What you should do is to wind off the lock, and that generally reduces the understeer. So remember, increase the lock and you increase the understeer, reduce the lock and reduce the understeer. Rather than coming off the throttle and then stabbing it again to try to induce oversteer to compensate, it is more effective simply to wind off the lock progressively as you go through the corner, balancing the understeer as it builds up. The less lock you have on, the less tyre punishment. Keep in mind that in a racing car understeer can usually be adjusted!

The point to remember is that the tyres perform at their optimum at very small angles of attack against the road. The fastest and most effective way round the circuit, with the minimum of tyre strain, will be reflected by a consistently light feel through the steering. If the steering starts feeling heavy you are putting the tyres and suspension through more than they were designed to deal with.

Summing up, if you go round a corner correctly the steering will feel light because the car is addressing the road surface at the right angle and is finding its way through the corner in the correct manner. Everything about its response feels very light: in other words, in this connection, 'if it's light, it's right'.

If, on the other hand, you go into the corner incorrectly, or on the wrong line, the steering gets very heavy. That means you are starting to scrub the tyres against the road, abusing the suspension and the whole car is complaining. It's the only way the car has of talking to you, of saying 'it's heavy, you've got it wrong', telling us when we, in fact, are driving in the incorrect fashion.

I have to stress that I differentiate between understeer and the American term 'pushing' and see them as two different characteristics in a racing car. Understeer can be an aerodynamic factor and a lack of front end grip. 'Push' can be an over-exuberance of rear-end grip which can drive the front end forward. It amounts to the same thing in the end, you might think, but sometimes the technique for changing the balance of the car can be a great deal more complicated.

Even with a car that is understeering, the 'cheap' and easy way of rectifying it is simply to make the rear-end grip less effective. That doesn't do the trick, because what you're doing is robbing Peter to pay Paul. All you end up with is a neutral-handling car, which feels nice to drive, but has no grip. You need to make both ends grip and both ends behave in a well balanced way.

Cars generally don't produce understeer on the immediate turn-in to a corner. They tend, on the initial turn of the wheel, to behave as if they are going to execute the corner as desired. So in those first fractions of a second while applying the car to the corner you think 'Ah, it's going to work perfectly'. But as it completes the first third of the corner it develops understeer in a progressive fashion. So what do you do?

You can either back off and get the rear end to kick out and power-slide it round the corner, or you can trim the car properly. In a fast corner it can be aerodynamic: it may be that you do not have sufficient downforce on the front end of the car. If that is the case, the situation can be adjusted by changing front and rear wing angles.

The problem could lie with cambers, roll bars, springs or dampers. There are occasions when you have to apply more roll stiffness and a stiffer spring rate, although generally one goes softer on roll bar, springs and dampers. These things have a tendency to defeat and confuse you because there are cars on which you can introduce too much roll. Let's say you have gone too soft on the front roll bar, you go round a corner and now it progressively begins to roll more and more, finally flopping over into what we call 'roll oversteer', the car torsionally twisting front-left corner to the right-rear corner on a right-hand bend, or front-right corner to left-rear corner on a left-hand bend.

From an understeering car it will suddenly be transformed into an

Handing over the Capri to François Cevert at Paul Ricard—those cars were really hard work!

oversteering car. That is the least agreeable of all, because the car's characteristics do not remain consistent throughout the duration of the corner and it usually occurs just before you apply the throttle.

If possible, killing the initial understeer should be done by mechanical means rather than solely by aerodynamics. Correcting understeer simply by putting more downforce on the front can produce a speed handicap on the straights and the car can start pivoting nervously round its front end, even on the slightest amount of steering input. Every time you go into a faster corner the car will over-respond to steering input causing the tail end to wag. This is something you try to avoid.

Try to go through the mechanical aspect. Think about going slightly softer on the front roll bar; not by a giant margin, but sufficient to enable you to notice the difference. It may be that you need to make the rear bar slightly stiffer, because it could be the lack of rear roll stiffness that is causing the car to plough on at the front – that is, driving the front on. This is what I would call 'push'. But don't go to such a stiff rear roll bar that the car will 'dirt track' round the corner in a big oversteering slide. That makes the rear end 'loose', to use the American phraseology.

Roll bar adjustment is a fairly easy and fast thing to do. When you set a car up to begin with, don't leave home with the roll bar at either extreme; set it to the centre of its range, so that you can adjust it quickly when you are at the track. That's just logical, you might think, but a lot of people don't do it. It's also important to have at least one other roll bar ('sway bar' in the US) of a different diameter and stiffness.

147

Springs are like roll bars – even at the most basic level of competition you should have a selection of them to choose from. It could be that you are driving a car with progressive-rate springs – softer through the initial movement and gradually stiffening as they go into compression. If you decide on softer front springs it will probably reduce an element of that understeer. But of course it's possible to go too far down this road and you then encounter a whole selection of other undesirable effects, such as not settling down on rebound, which means that the car does not recover from bumps or undulations quickly.

Another element of understeer which can be potentially misleading is when the suspension movement is too soft owing to a driver, after finding himself in an understeer situation, over-softening the front roll bar. dampers and springs. Now the car can reach the suspension bump rubbers – the rubber blocks which limit suspension movement to prevent the car touching the ground. In these conditions the car will be riding on those bump rubbers on heavy braking and, of course, cornering. When the car turns into the corner there is nowhere for the suspension to move. It's as hard as an old nail and will simply understeer even more. A lot of people believe that they will get more bite at the front end by softening the front bar, but they go far too far and introduce another form of understeer as a result.

If you soften up the front end too much on springs, shock absorbers and roll bars, you can still suffer from understeer. This is because you have produced a car which is too sloppy and too soft to force its front tyres firmly on the road. Understeer can occur just as much by setting the car too softly at the front as by being too hard.

The next point to consider is oversteer. In my early club racing days oversteer was dealt with quite simply by adjusting tyre pressures. Thinking back to my young days, to a little go-kart I used to drive from time to time, is amusing. It was logical to me as a very young person that you would get more grip if you deflated the tyres because you would get more rubber in contact with the road. That's how it seemed to me at the time.

I soon learned that this was incorrect, but you have to go through all these learning processes for yourself, and it's not inconceivable that somebody reading this book today might be thinking along the same lines. Of course, there is no purpose in inflating a tyre to the point where it develops a crown and is only wearing down the centre rather than evenly across the whole tread. In simple terms, a little more pressure can produce extra grip through tyre stability; which may be of help to competitors at basic club level, and of significance to the 'showroom stock' categories which are becoming extremely popular in the USA and require the use of showroom tyres, available over the counter to the public.

When one gets further up the competition ladder, dealing with cars equipped with adjustable suspension, the most commonly worked area is the anti-roll bar, and the rear roll bar in particular. It tends to be adjustments to the rear roll bar which are made primarily, simply because it's usually easier to reach and to change than the front anti-roll bar.

If you've got oversteer, it's likely that you want to soften the rear roll bar, weakening its torsional strength, so as to give you a little more grip at the back end. You must also be aware that if the car has become too soft at the front end, it can pivot round the front wheels, as if it's nailed to the road with the rear wagging round in a relatively uncontrollable fashion. So don't think that the loose rear end feeling is necessarily caused solely by the rear adjustments. It can come from the front end too.

A driver has to compartmentalise the car in his thoughts, to be able to analyse the sequence of adjustments to rectify the problem. If softening the rear bar doesn't improve matters, the driver should go back to the original rear setting and consider something else. It is very important to do one change at a time. Then there is the question of springs and the bump rubbers at the rear: if the suspension goes onto the bump rubbers at the rear it will suddenly make the car kick out in an abrupt fashion. That is a very strange feeling, and one which is both uncomfortable and unpredictable.

The one thing you don't want is unpredictable oversteer. With understeer you can always back off the throttle and restore some semblance of control. But unpredictable oversteer can really be a problem, because you can be right on your limit when it whips away from you. And even if you take your foot off the throttle at that point it could, in some cases, increase your problem.

Most cars can be worked into a reasonable state of balance between front and rear, although I have experienced some during my career that have been beyond 'help'. As I've said before, when I was in the Tyrrell team we were never able to get a car at Brands Hatch that I found I could make work properly. That was the one place where I always had to drive round problems.

I feel that this was as much my fault as it was the team's. I seemed to be incapable of sorting out a car to ride the bumps and undulations at Brands Hatch correctly, and I found it was just about the most difficult track in the world for me to set up a car for. The best car I ever drove round there was a Ferrari 330 P4 sports car which I drove in the World Championship of Makes decider run at the circuit, the 1967 BOAC 100 km.

I shared this P4 with Chris Amon, driving for the works team. An interesting sideline is that I was asked by both Porsche and Ferrari to drive there: they were looking to tie up all the best drivers because they were both trying for the World Championship. Porsche, in fact, asked me first, but it wasn't Huschke von Hanstein, the team manager at that time, who called me up but his secretary. She asked if I would drive for the team, I replied that it was possible, I would look into it and so forth, so would she please call me back later.

I was driving for BRM at the time and I discussed it with them, of course, and I came back and agreed in principle. Von Hanstein's secretary had told me that Jochen Rindt, Bruce McLaren and Graham Hill were all going to drive, and that I shouldn't be left out of it. She then called me back, as agreed, and I asked what the driving fee would be on this occasion.

She said, 'Money? It's an honour to drive for Porsche!' Honestly, that was her response! I told her, 'Well I'm a Scotsman, not a German and I'm a professional racing driver and I would expect to be paid, as I would for driving any to her car for any other team!' So I went off and arranged to drive the Ferrari. Huschke later came back and apologised, said the secretary had misunderstood and we could of course arrange something. I told him not to bother, that I had made other arrangements to drive for Ferrari.

So it was quite interesting that my drive with Chris produced enough points to clinch the World Championship of Makes for Ferrari ahead of Porsche, although we only finished second to Phil Hill and Mike Spence in the Chaparral. What I do recall about that race was that Chris was sick, really unwell in the car, but it was a very enjoyable drive otherwise and my first experience of driving a car that really worked well at Brands. Chris

Possibly the best handling car I ever drove at Brands Hatch was the Ferrari 330P4 sports prototype which I shared with Chris Amon in the 1967 BOAC 1000 kms race. We finished second to the Chaparral and clinched the sports car title for Ferrari.

and I worked very hard setting up that P4 with Mauro Forghieri. In fact, it is one of the regrets of my racing career that I was never able to work with Forghieri on a long-term basis.

I nearly did sign for Ferrari on a couple of occasions during my career and one of the factors which attracted me to the team was the prospect of working with Mauro Forghieri. At that time, in the late 1960s, he was certainly the man who was sorting out chassis development for them. Anyway, that was the first time I got a car to work properly at Brands which at that time was one of the bumpiest tracks in the business.

I never won a British Grand Prix at Brands, although I won a couple of non-Championship races and I also won in a Lotus Elan and a Formula 3 car. But I didn't win a Formula 2 race and I can recall being blown off by Jack Sears' Willment Cobra when I was driving John Coombs' Jaguar E-type in a sports car race supporting the 1964 British Grand Prix.

So despite winning those non-Championship races, one in a Matra and one in a March, somehow or other I never felt comfortable at the place. It was a track for which you had to have a lot of suspension, wheel movement, bump and rebound control. If you get a car which hasn't got a good combination of springs and dampers, a car which has a lot of camber change, the car is 'darty' and moves all over the road.

At places like the old Nürburgring, these qualities were also of crucial importance, particularly before the circuit was resurfaced in 1971 and became the 'clinical' old Nürburgring. In those days, when the old circuit was at the peak of its challenge and danger, the driver carried the car around the track: it was obviously a great help to have a car that worked, but ultimately it was down to the driver. Some of those early laps at the old 'Ring' will always go down in my mind as the ultimate driver challenge. There was nothing else in the history of motor racing, in my view, that came close to the Nürburgring although I'm sure some people might suggest otherwise and cite endurance events like the Targa Florio or the Mille Miglia. But, in my opinion, nobody ever raced in those events to the ultimate potential of either themselves or the cars because the individual laps and the races were so long.

The Nürburgring was bad enough at just over 14 miles to a lap, and precious few ever drove there at the ultimate limit of their ability, but nevertheless it was leaping and jumping, taking off and flying a long way some 13 times per lap. You went to the 'Ring' with a car stacked up with bump rubbers to stop it grinding itself to nothing by bottoming out.

That may seem a long way from the basics of oversteer, but there was change in the late 1960s and early 1970s when we started to adjust chassis behaviour by aerodynamic means. Although, aerodynamically we were still very much in the dark, during these early years, it was a particularly interesting era because we were not only coming from narrow tyres to the big wide 'doughnuts', but also from virgin aerodynamics to highly sophisticated techniques.

When the aerodynamic era arrived we were talking in terms of pop-riveting little fins onto the front nose cone of the Matra MS10 and that was all we had. Then we put a funny little wing on the back – those early attempts at attaching wings were really quite amusing. They then developed through the 'big wing' and 'bi-plane' era. Of course, what finally stopped this particular route were the accidents to Graham Hill and Jochen Rindt during the Spanish Grand Prix at Montjuich Park, Barcelona in 1969. The sport's governing body, the CSI as it was in those days, consequently suddenly banned wings. There was a great furore about that!

Of course wings came back, but with better regulations governing their dimensions and structure.

On the whole, though, nobody was really certain what they were doing in the business of cleaning up the car from an aerodynamic point of view. Wind tunnels had not really been used for racing car development at that time and few of the Grand Prix designers had come from the aerospace world. We were shooting in the dark: there were no end plates on the wings, for example. When they were fitted, that was a big step forward as it prevented aerodynamic 'spill' over the side of the aerofoils, although what the turbulence was like over those cars must have been something else. It was a period of near black magic for a while.

It is also instructive to consider the differences involved between balancing a single-seater and a touring car, although I didn't do much touring car racing in the latter part of my career.

Coming from single-seaters to touring cars was always a very enjoyable experience for me. The car was so much more forgiving than driving a single-seater which was such a precise, highly strung, nervous machine. The switch to a sliding, forgiving device was sheer fun.

One of my most vivid recollections of that feeling was when I drove a Broadspeed Escort in the 1970 Tourist Trophy at Silverstone, sharing the car with Chris Craft. It was a particularly difficult time in my life when I had just come from the memorial service for Bruce McLaren and the burial of Piers Courage. I was just fed up with motor racing. I simply didn't want to do it anymore.

So I went to Silverstone to drive that Escort. What fun it was, God knows what the tyre temperatures were! The car was sideways most of the way round the circuit, but I felt an exuberance with my childhood pleasure in handling a car returning to me, and it was so nice to be able to do it. It was not always like that, however, and it's not quite like that today, because by 1973 I was, of course, driving almostly exclusively in Grands Prix. I had given up Indianapolis and Can-Am, but then I came out of my 'non-Grand Prix retirement' to drive a few races in a Ford Capri for Mike Kranefuss's Ford Cologne competitions department in the European Touring Car Championship.

Emerson Fittipaldi and I did Monza and the Nürburgring, François Cevert did Paul Ricard with me. The cars were so heavy, so difficult to drive, I just can't begin to describe it! It was such a big challenge. Here were the so-called 'ace' drivers, Emerson and I, and here were the young lions – Jochen Mass, Hans Heyer, Dieter Glemser and Niki Lauda . . . we were clay pigeons out there to be shot at!

The young boys went all out to demonstrate their virtuosity and incredible talent over those two established Grand Prix stars, so whatever we did, it was wrong. If we were faster, well, of course, we ought to be . . . if we were slower, it was . . . 'look at the young guy, he's faster than Fittipaldi or Stewart'. We were on a hiding to nothing in whichever direction we wished to travel.

We had a lot of fun, but our arms were not strong enough to steer the cars! The amount of effort was unbelievable: it was like turning the clock back to the old Lotus Cortina days, on three wheels and two. I'll never forget arriving at the Nürburgring and getting blown off by the young guys; and this was at a time when I thought I drove the Nürburgring quite well. But I could not lap faster than Jochen Mass, although he was on Dunlops and I was on Goodyears because of my F1 contract. What a nightmare.

Finally, I said 'It must be the tyres', so we swapped cars. Jochen went out and was still three seconds a lap quicker than me – and I was nine seconds a lap faster than Emerson. They were just so much better than us in those cars. There is a photograph taken by Walter Hayes when I got out of the car after my first stint in the race and there was a cloud of steam coming off my overalls. I was that exhausted. Luckily, Emerson broke the car during the second stint, which was a great relief to me!

This was something of a contrast to my earliest experience in touring car competition. Way back I had driven a Jaguar 3.8 litre saloon in club races at Charterhall, a car owned by Hugh Patrick, a local Glasgow enthusiast. We had Dunlop racing tyres, Koni shock absorbers, platinum-plated distributor points and sparking plugs, and we took the air cleaners off.

I think I had a four-point seat harness and a special bucket seat, which we got from Jaguar Cars. All I can recall is that it was very fast. We didn't do anything in the way of changing springs or dampers, although I remember that we broke the rear Panhard rod on a regular basis on Charterhall's bumpy surface.

The next touring car I drove was a Lotus Cortina for Charles Bridges of Red Rose Motors – we had it with the Stewart tartan stripe down the side instead of the normal green one. That was such a bad-handling car. The first one was an Alan Mann team car I had tried at Goodwood in 1964 and it was so bad that I just couldn't believe it. Everybody laughed at me because they had all agreed that I would come in and insist that there was something wrong with it.

It was great for me to experience a wide variety of competition cars early in my career and in 1964 I drove no fewer than 26 cars in 53 races. But the Lotus Cortina was one massive compromise: there was nothing you could change on it. You bought it and that was it, and at that time it was quite something to get your hands on one in the first place. Charles Bridges had to say that he was going to have Jackie Stewart driving it, and I was the most successful club driver of the previous year and so on.

I wish he had never got it. It was terrible. I was also given the chance of handling the Ecurie Ecosse Cooper-Monaco and their Tojeiro Buick so there was a great diversity of machinery available and I developed a degree of versatility which was very important. If a driver is on the way up, I do believe that he should get as many rides as possible in a broad selection of cars. At the end of the day, 'What have you won recently?' is the crucial question which you will be asked.

These were great challenges which taught me a lot, working with different mechanics and different teams and, of course, totally different cars.

Returning to the main thrust of the high-performance technique, I have always believed that racing in the rain really sorts out the men from the boys. The good, smooth driver will generally come out better in the wet, although there have been a few exceptions to this rule.

Wet-weather driving requires a rare delicacy of touch, although sometimes it is possible to see a 'car control' merchant really shining in the wet, generally on slow circuits.

On the average circuit, about 20 seconds a lap is the difference between dry and wet conditions. Curiously, straightline speed differs very little, although you have to apply the power very much more progressively, and that, in a way, helps teach you to become a better driver.

There are two or three things that you've got to avoid, of course. Really late braking is one: you can lock up the wheels and you don't have the room to sort the situation out as you have in the dry. In this connection I firmly

To the victor the spoils; twice World Champion Nelson Piquet on the victory rostrum after the 1986 Brazilian Grand Prix.

believe that anti-lock ABS braking systems will eventually be adopted in many forms of motor sport: in fact, I'm rather surprised it hasn't come about already. I know that people suggest that it might impose a weight penalty on the car, but I don't think this is very relevant. I suspect the reluctance to adopt them has stemmed from a macho-type 'we can always do better than ABS' kind of attitude which may not necessarily be true in principle – and certainly is not true as far as some individual drivers are concerned. The additional weight penalty imposed by anti-lock is minimal when compared with the systems advantages.

You use less road in the rain; you don't use the full width of the race track. If you do, you tend to run into pools of water. The moment you hit one of those it breaks away or hooks up in deep water and certainly causes you a great deal of aggravation, and possibly much worse.

To deal with wet conditions you need a softer-sprung car. You have to slacken off roll bars, spring rates and damper settings. You want the car to be supple, more 'grippy' in every way. It's well worth a driver developing a car in the rain. A short wheelbase car is a lot more darty in the rain; a long wheelbase car is preferable. If I was going racing again today I would have a specially prepared wet-weather car which would only be rolled out in the rain, but it would be so much better than a car which was a compromise for wet/dry conditions that I would win a couple of Grands Prix a year just on the strength of that.

It would be a more forgiving car, softer sprung, with different aerodynamics and a revised brake balance, incorporating all the elements that I would work out during controlled wet-weather testing which, at the present time, is not being done by anybody in the F1 business.

This variety is invaluable and gives you an insight into the difficulties and challenges of running in different categories like this. For example, just as I had found with the Capris back in 1973, in 1984 Martin Brundle was telling me that driving the Jaguar XJS coupés in the European Touring Car Championship was a hugely different experience from driving his Formula 1 Tyrrell – and that the people who drive them regularly are specialists who drive very well indeed and are very difficult to beat.

The other crucial aspect which you can learn a great deal about from driving in another catetory is the importance of detailed preparation. I was always extremely hot on having the cockpit of my cars as tidy and as clean as they could possibly be. I didn't like to see loose wires hanging down all over the place. They should at least be taped together or preferably tucked away in a tube out of sight. I quite recently had the opportunity to drive one of the factory Porsche 956's – a good, forgiving car which I suspect many people can drive very competitively relatively easily – and I have to say that I was not particularly impressed with the standard of detail finish in the cockpit. I felt that there should have been a great deal more sorbo rubber around components such as the steering rack, to protect the drivers' legs from being unduly bashed about. This sort of thing is obviously an area in which the driver has to take an active interest as well, but it was surprising that a team with Porsche's experience had not already taken the initiative on this without any prompting.

Everything should be immaculate in the cockpit – and, for that matter, everywhere else. I hate to see cars with wheels that are not clean on the inside, or tyre sidewalls that are not blacked. Dirty cars tend to suggest that the mechanics are either sloppy, or they have not had sufficient time to prepare it. You only have to take one look at a car to see what its detail preparation has been like. You cannot only blame the mechanics because their performance is frequently a reflection of the standards displayed by the team manager and driver.

As an aside, it is perhaps worth recalling one telling episode from my early racing days when I was testing one of Ken Tyrrell's Formula 2 Matras at Goodwood. As I went into St Mary's I lifted off to steady the car, and nothing happened. When I tried to brake nothing happened either. I switched off the ignition and went plunging across the grass, rejoining the track almost on the Lavant Straight which brought me back down towards the pits. I was tremendously fortunate that I didn't hit anything and that the car didn't turn over . . .

On closer examination we found that one of the mechanics had left a spanner in the footwell, lying between the pedals in such a way that I could neither apply the brakes nor close the throttle. It was a frightening testimony to the need for meticulous preparation. Another time, I might not have been so lucky.

It is easy to make a car handle in the rain which, at the same time will be moderately good in the dry. But I can make a car work very well in the dry which will be terrible in the rain. For road driving, therefore, I would always do the majority of my research and development work in wet-weather conditions. On the road, more than 90 per cent of all serious injuries and fatalities occur in wet or slippery conditions. I would therefore set most of the parameters of the car to deal with those requirements.

The result would be a car that handled very nicely and comfortably in the dry. At the present time most car manufacturers set their cars up to cope with the dry, so when it rains many of them are not at all good to drive and can induce problems that could be avoided. A philosophical change of attitude is definitely required within the motor industry.

Chapter 5
What We Learn

Tyres are the easiest and most obvious aspect to consider in this section. I think the acceleration of knowledge in passenger tyre development, both in terms of original equipment and for the replacement market, has been helped considerably by racing. Detroit, Tokyo and the world's other motor industry capitals are increasingly confronted by government regulations and market requirements that can be extremely challenging for the engineers involved.

For example, in the USA the designers are faced with having to deal with the CAFE regulations which are a set of mandatory government rules applied to each manufacturer requiring a certain Corporate Average Fuel Economy. This means that General Motors or Ford or Chrysler have to produce their complete range of cars to average out at around, say, 27 mpg. That means if you have a 7-litre gas guzzler in your line-up it will probably kill the entire range as it will be very difficult for the smaller engined cars to balance it out. What's more, the fines imposed for failing to meet the requirements of these regulations are so enormous that no efforts are spared to ensure that the correct consumption figures are achieved.

That may seem a long way from being a tyre-maker's problem. However, when the tyre-maker is approached by the original equipment client (the car manufacturer) and told, 'We need a tyre with less rolling resistance for good fuel consumption, but want excellent traction and good mileage on tyre wear', it becomes his problem. So what are you going to do? Everybody has been asking for wider tyres which improve the car's cosmetic appearance and have larger 'footprints' to cope with the new demands on handling which have entered the American market, but this makes it less easy to attain good fuel economy.

In years gone by, the American motor industry never built a car which really handled well in the European sense of the word. Then suddenly the second fuel crisis came along and imported cars began to make major inroads into the domestic American market because they were smaller, lighter and, of course, had better fuel consumption. The Americans got used to driving smaller cars which, for the first time in their experience, went in the direction they were pointed.

Previously, the American motorist had been driving round in a vehicle which resembled more a sitting room than a car: it was overweight, oversized, over-plush, covered with superflous embellishments, clumsy and it handled like a pregnant elephant.

The US manufacturers' reaction to this new competition was to put bigger wheels and tyres on their reduced-size models in an attempt to

Tyre technology is the most obvious area in which competition input helps us to produce a better product for the road car. Here I am strapped into the cockpit of a Chevy Corvette during a development run at Akron.

improve handling. But those wider wheels and tyres meant more rolling resistance: it is more difficult to push the car along when it has more rubber on the road and is generating more surface friction. So people said, 'OK, we'll make a harder compound, therefore you'll have a wider tyre and better mileage on tyre wear yet still have good fuel consumption'. That worked until the rain came and then the hard compound slipped all over the place as it had no grip. It proved extremely difficult to produce a tyre design and compound which was an acceptable compromise.

I know with the work I do for Goodyear that this is one of the major issues which has been addressed and many of the compounders who were involved in the racing department are now the compounders working on original equipment passenger car tyres, trying to get that rolling resistance factor married to adhesion and to footprint and styling. That has been an enormously important element in the tyre-maker's challenge to satisfy not just the car makers but also government requirements. So these engineers have been exercised to the limits of their ability in this gymnasium which we call motor sport. They are fitter, stronger, more agile, on the lookout for better alternatives, keeping in mind all the latest, constantly-changing requirements.

Since the advent of the ground-effect aerodynamics era in Formula 1 – and in subsequent high-downforce configurations in other formulae – another aspect of suspension performance was introduced to the technical equation. The tyres, because of the very small wheel and suspension movement involved, have become an integral part of that suspension system. In other words, the sidewall of the tyres is being used to accommodate some of the track/car movement, which had not been originally envisaged as a function of the modern racing tyre.

To be specific and relating this to high-performance road tyres, we have a 70 series tyre, with a 70 aspect ratio (the ratio between tyre sidewall height and tread width) which has quite a high sidewall. But we have subsequently developed the 65, then the 60, the 50 and the 45 aspect ratio.

The lower the aspect ratio of the tyre, the shallower the sidewall and the less cushioning effect it has – therefore more shock and road reaction can be transmitted through it. The most extreme example of this in original equipment terms was when the Chevrolet Corvette was marketed in the early 1980s fitted with the low profile Goodyear Eagle tyre, dubbed the 'gator back'. It featured the directional tread pattern which had been developed specifically for General Motors. This was perhaps the first occasion when a tyre manufacturer had worked exclusively on a single project with a car manufacturer.

The car was far too harsh on those tyres for normal everyday road use. For me, this signalled the arrival of the American motor industry's first major attempt at making a car handle competitively with anything that the rest of the world could produce. But they went much too far: too hard on suspension – certainly for my taste – and the car was a boneshaker.

Unfortunately the story doesn't end there, because now the cars are now out of guarantee, and some will have arrived on the used car market. It's quite possible that they will be rather on the loose side because they may have had a good shaking.

Similarly, you can see Mercedes-Benz 500 SECs, Volkswagen Golf GTIs and so on which have been modified by non-factory specialists, whose terribly low suspension and low aspect ratio tyres make the cars far too rigid, in my view. It's interesting to note that Chevrolet did in fact produce a car which surpassed even a Porsche 928 in terms of lateral G-force figures

160

continued on page 177

Wet conditions catch out even the most experienced! The importance of delicate throttle control in the wet is underlined by Nelson Piquet spinning his Brabham-BMW BT54 in the middle of the pack on the opening corner of the 1985 Belgian Grand Prix at Spa.

Even the most minor excursions can store up problems for the future and it is crucially important to react correctly at such times. Nigel Mansell's Williams-Honda slides very wide at Druids hairpin on the opening lap of the 1985 Grand Prix of Europe, Brands Hatch. He was able to coax his machine off the dirt successfully and went on to win the race but his trip onto the dust and dirt off-line could well have resulted in tyre damage (left).

Russell Spence's Reynard 853 bumps the chicane kerb at Zolder, an understandable touch of over-exuberance on the part of the 1985 Grovewood Award winner but not to be recommended as a regular technique (inset). Neither is the treatment being meted out to Johansson's Ferrari as it straddles the kerbing after spinning off following engine failure at Spa in 1985 (overleaf).

LAT PHOTOGRAPHIC

NIGEL SNOWDON

Hard work! This shot of Kyle Petty's Ford Thunderbird on the Daytona banking indicates the sort of G-forces and consequent wear and tear which has to be sustained by NASCAR stock drivers. If anybody argues that motor racing is not a truly athletic activity, a stint in one of these sweat boxes should change their opinion! (inset)

Nigel Mansell's Lotus 95T glances one of the unyielding concrete walls which lined the course of the 1984 Dallas Grand Prix. The need for absolute concentration and precision is paramount on such tracks (left).

167

Flag signals provide the racing driver with his only outside source of information about track conditions. They should be obeyed scrupulously as most marshals display very high standards of competence (above).

Delicate throttle control as well as the need to leave bigger margins for potential error are prime requirements for wet-weather driving. Alain Prost (previous page) shows Championship style as he slithers towards victory in the 1984 Monaco Grand Prix, while (right) Nigel Mansell and Keke Rosberg show similar sensitivity tip-toeing round Spa in their Williams-Hondas.

Even the top drivers get it wrong: Keke Rosberg locks up his Williams prior to spinning off at Kyalami in 1985. Mansell, following, has just enough time to avoid the error (above).

Mansell's Williams bottoms out in a shower of sparks on his way to victory in the 1985 Grand Prix of Europe at Brands Hatch. The sparks are coming from the skid plates beneath the car which are provided to protect the underside of the chassis (right).

Philippe Streiff giving his Ligier a hard time over the kerbing during the 1985 Australian Grand Prix . . . something to avoid!

I admire the way in which Ayrton Senna has developed a (usually) meticulous driving technique early in his career with Lotus (right). But he still shows signs of youthful exuberance as he bangs a wheel up the kerb trying to muscle ahead of Rosberg at the start of the 1985 Italian Grand Prix (above).

continued from page 160

developed when cornering hard on a constant radius circle. But that does not mean to say that it was appropriate for the kind of utilisation by the sort of people who buy a Corvette in America.

In my opinion, the car's suspension did not suit it to the kind of urban conditions found in New York City, Chicago and Philadelphia, for example, where severe winters have caused road surfaces to be damaged by potholes and undulations. Incidentally, in my experience, American road maintenance does not come up to the standards seen in European countries.

The science of tyre making is going through a very exciting period. Motor racing has always contributed to the accelerated rate of tyre development – more obviously, perhaps, than in any other area of car dynamics. But what we are really looking for is a tyre which will accommodate a great many qualities because in a road car environment we are concerned with styling, with fuel efficiency through low rolling resistance, road feel, shock transfer, sound deadening and, not least, grip.

For road purposes, though, a high-performance tyre must necessarily be a compromise. My ideal road tyre would be something that provided a 70 aspect ratio ride for comfort with a 50 aspect ratio level of grip and sensitivity. Now, because of the new materials and know-how coming into the high technology tyre development programmes, we are fast approaching the time when we will be able to produce that kind of commodity.

So tyre technology in motor sport has been a major contributor towards finding the talent to undertake those kinds of projects which have sometimes amounted to emergency priority when assisting the car manufacturer through all the regulations requirements.

Goodyear spend considerable sums of money on research and development and their technical centres are very extensive indeed. In addition to Goodyear there are high-performance products from BF Goodrich, Yokohama, Bridgestone, Pirelli, Michelin, Firestone, Dunlop and others. Many of these companies are using racing expertise and knowledge in the production of their tyres.

I do a lot of tyre testing and Goodyear has set up a small specialist 'tactical force' to concentrate on this and other special areas of development. And we're coming out with a tyre development programme which is almost identical to what I did as a racing driver. I go about my passenger tyre testing in exactly the same way as I went testing at Kyalami, or Paul Ricard, or Silverstone. Many of the engineers working with this small group – and there are only ten or twelve – have come from a racing environment.

They have either been designers or compounders and are a highly skilled group. But I am using exactly the same analysis techniques as I did when I was racing, no matter whether I am testing a new compound, stiffer belting, new materials inside the carcass, a revised construction, a new sidewall or a new profile. We do the tests at Akron, Luxembourg, at Miravel in the south of France and San Angelo in Texas. In every case, motor racing has helped to a very significant degree in formulating the methods we use to carry out these programmes.

Aerodynamics is another important area where motor racing has helped production car development. Think of the air dams which have been brought in over recent years to help the front-end downforce, not only assisting steering response but also providing good penetration. The improved aerodynamic performance helps reduce fuel consumption of passenger vehicles.

In these views of me tyre testing for Goodyear at Akron, I am using the latest model Chevrolet Corvette. In the cockpit with me in the main picture is Tim Coconis, one of the youngsters I have been introducing to the development driving 'task force' within Goodyear's development programme.

Everything which is done today is measured in apparently minuscule percentage terms. But if you make a four per cent improvement, that is a giant positive stride towards meeting the CAFE fuel consumption requirements. In that respect the aerodynamicist has, in many cases, overtaken the stylist in terms of overall importance when formulating the outline design of a road car.

If we look back 15 or 20 years the stylist was, to a large degree, simply creating embellishments. Now the stylist is removing every unnecessary object, cleaning up the car from every point of view. Look at the Ford Sierra, the Audi, the Mercedes, the Porsche or the Ford Thunderbird in America; those cars are very clean aerodynamically. But it's interesting that America stayed longer than any other country with the old-fashioned, square-cut, box-shaped profile, remaining almost alone in this respect after the rest of the world's motor industry had gone aerodynamic, concentrating on CD (coefficient of drag) figures as a number one priority.

As I write this book today, some of the Detroit manufacturers are still locked into what I call the 'Old Apple Pie' look, which, frankly, is out of place and out of step with the rest of the world. Nevertheless, there is a large core of buyers in America which has been brought up with that look and sees no good reason for changing it. Of course, these cars would not sell anywhere else in the world, so perhaps this is why Ford is doing so well in the US market place at present, drawing on its international experience in the worldwide market which tells it that the aerodynamic route is the one to follow.

Suspension development is another area to consider – shock absorbers,

for example. Motor racing has taught us a great deal about the benefits of gas-filled dampers. They don't aerate or lose their efficiency anywhere near as quickly as oil-filled types. The current high level of braking performance on road cars can also largely be traced back to progress made in motor sport circles, although one of the greatest technical contributions for several decades is the evolution of anti-lock braking. This feature is now standard for the entire Ford Granada range, for example, and in the Lincoln Mark 7 in the US while Audi, BMW and Mercedes-Benz also offer similar options within their product ranges. This is a great safety factor which didn't come from motor racing at all, illustrating, perhaps, that we cannot take credit for every aspect of improved performance. In fact I prophesy that it will be brought into racing in due course.

The quite remarkable progress made in aerodynamics can be gauged by contrasting the Sierra RS Cosworth and the current Granada Scorpio with the old square-cut Zodiac Mk 4 from the late Sixties and its predecessor the Mk 3 (overleaf).

However, it would be wrong to underrate the contribution made by motor racing in many varied areas. Some of these contributions have been very simple; for a long time in motor sport we have been working with windscreens which do not reflect the instruments up into the driver's line of vision. This goes back to experience gained in long-distance events such as Le Mans, where it was of paramount importance not to have distractions of that nature cropping up when driving at high speed during the night! With the new aero shapes, the windscreens on road cars are presenting similar problems that can be dealt with through experience.

Lubricants should be considered as well. When I was working with Elf in the early 1970s we had a soluble synthetic oil which we actually raced. The involvement of companies such as Elf, Mobil and Shell motor sport have meant the development of more efficient lubricants which, in turn, make

The Mk 3 Zodiac (right) and its Mk 4 successor (above) were the products of stylists, not aerodynamicists.

The increased emphasis placed on aerodynamic integrity also holds good in North America, witness the dramatic contrast between the 1983 Ford Thunderbird (in front of which I am standing) and the over-ornate Mercury Cougar from 1967 (overleaf).

their contribution towards saving fuel by reducing frictional losses within the engine and in other components which require specialist friction-free lubrication.

A lot of people simply believe that motor racing is a gas-guzzling exercise, but that's not true at all. If you had started a race with no thought for fuel consumption in the days prior to the current Formula 1 195-litre (42.9 Imperial gallons/51.5 US gallons) maximum rule you might well have found yourself in a position where you were carrying more fuel than your rivals and your car would was heavier, less agile and less competitive in the early part of the race. A good engine burns its fuel efficiently to provide the best possible performance for the job in hand. In racing that means manageable, reliable horsepower with whatever amount of fuel is permitted,

I think it is also worth recognising the sort of technology and knowledge accumulated over the years by companies such as Cosworth Engineering, who built both the Ford DFV which powered me to my three championships in addition to the brand new turbocharged Ford V6 engine which made its Formula 1 debut in 1986. Not only has Cosworth's know-how been harnessed to develop production car versions for Ford and GM, but they have produced a four-valve cylinder head for the Mercedes-Benz 190. In the same way, Porsche has accumulated considerable technical knowledge over the years from its continuing competition programme, to the point where between 45 and 50 per cent of the firm's overall revenue comes from research and development work carried out for outside clients.

Turbocharging is another area where racing has unquestionably improved the breed. The turbocharger in itself is not exclusively a product of racing, but the efficiency of the turbocharger, the acceleration of turbo technology and knowledge, has largely come from motor sport. You only have to consider just how uncompetitive the first 1.5-litre Formula 1 turbocharged Renault was in its early days, with its problems of poor response, particularly in traffic and in the rain, to appreciate the enormous strides which have been made over the past several years. Now the 1.5-litre turbo is very workable, very driveable and so much faster than a normally aspirated engine that they made the poor old 3-litre Ford-Cosworth V8 redundant.

Renault, perhaps naturally, was one of the first companies to exploit the turbo concept in production road cars, while more recently Ford has taken a leaf out of its American racing programme by using a turbocharged engine with electronic fuel injection which has been transferred to the SVO Mustang.

Of course, aside from specific technical areas, there are more general considerations which are worth bearing in mind. These include the sharpening up of the engineers' approach, the whole high-technology aura which association with a competition programme produces. Yet, surprisingly perhaps, there is still a remarkable amount of in-built resistance to competition programmes in some areas of the motor industry.

There is still an 'old brigade' which fails to see any benefit or sense coming from it all. Sometimes when I go testing at Dearborn I get people coming up saying 'I don't know what you guys are carrying on about, don't you know there is a 55 mph limit here?' What they don't understand is that when I'm testing and developing a new chassis, for example, I've got to test that chassis to the absolute limit of its ability, so I know what ultimate characteristics the chassis displays. And, if it has a bad character, it is often only on its limit that those poor qualities are going to become evident.

The 1967 Mercury Cougar–not pleasing by the aerodynamic standards of the Eighties.

186

So I have to drive to my personal limit, the car's limit, the tyres' limit, because once or twice in a buyer's lifetime they are going to need that car to react under extreme circumstances to prevent an accident. It may be to avoid a young child running out from behind a parked car, a cyclist or a motor cyclist. And it has to respond once to avoid, and again to recover from that avoidance. If those qualities do not exist, we will have done an enormous disservice to road users. That is why a chassis, ride and handling engineer has to drive so quickly to identify the car's true character at the limit, while at the same time combining all the other compromises which

187

have to be made. You can't have the suspension too hard and taut, too stiff on roll, because it has got to accommodate people comfortably within its interior without shaking them up with too harsh a ride.

A lot of my work involves helping to finalise the chassis specification of various road cars in the Ford range and, to this end, a lot of the Ford development engineers have attended courses at Bob Bondurant's High Performance Driving School, enabling them to develop a much fuller understanding of car and chassis behaviour on the limit. Obviously they are only at the start of their experience, but I would rather have a small amount of knowledge in this area than no knowledge at all, and I'm very glad that the company has seen fit to send them there. Even the Chairman

Production car handling has reached new levels of excellence in Europe, largely as a result of competition experience and now the American market has accepted the front-wheel drive Escort with enthusiasm.

of the Board, Donald Petersen, and the President of the company, Red Poling, have attended. They both drive extremely well and are very enthusiastic drivers, but I am sure they would concede that their driving techniques have improved thanks to that course.

This whole high-performance area is relatively new, particularly to the United States. It used to be that if you mentioned high-performance, all you were talking about was muscle power, of a 427 Mustang or something of that nature. Now we are considering the whole approach of high-performance motoring on a more sophisticated platform. We have, all around us, a wide cross-section of companies benefiting from involvement in competition motoring activities of one sort or another, from General Motors and Ford on both sides of the Atlantic, to Porsche, to Mercedes-Benz and, of course, BMW and Audi, the French, the Italians, the British and the Japanese. All of them have learned something positive from those involvements, and it shows.

We should also touch on the subject of the ergonomics of the driver's compartment, the whole package of an interior, considering particularly the driving controls – windscreen wipers, radios or indicators or instruments. Motor racing has always simplified those matters. It has often been in the mind of the road car designer that the fascia must be as impressive as possible, quite often with as many dials as you can fit in to make it look even more high-tech, but in the future that trend might change towards having only warning lights and warning sounds, rather than pressure gauges and temperature gauges all over the place.

If you contrast the difference between some of the cars which have carried my registration 1 JYS over the past twenty years or so, you'll get a good picture of the trend. In 1965 I owned a Jaguar S-type which had a great bank of switches and gauges ranged across the centre of its fascia. All very impressive, but the Ford Granada Scorpio I use in 1986 provides much better driving information from a far less cluttered instrument panel. Helen was expecting our son Paul when we had an Austin 1100. I had to put extensions on the switches on the dashboard because, in pregnancy, she could not reach them. I don't think that need happen today!

We are being told at the moment by design research analysts that the buying public still want things to look at, but if Mercedes-Benz or Porsche should introduce an uncomplicated instrument console, it will soon come to be regarded as the latest benchmark by which others are judged. This rather like telling the car-buying public 'let us make the cars to the best of our ability'; in other words, the butcher, the baker and the candlestick-maker are very well qualified to cut meat, cook bread and make candles, but as far as designing a safe and efficient car is concerned, we can help you with our knowledge and experience, just as other tradesmen do in their fields of expertise.

There are many instances when it has taken a Mercedes-Benz or a Porsche to take this sort of step. It is a risk to take it in the volume market, because the customer can just turn round and effectively say 'in that case we'll have one which we're used to from another manufacturer'. That can scare management. It's a slow process of evolution, therefore.

Since the lessons we have learned from competition motoring have now enabled manufacturers to produce cars which will go round corners more efficiently than their predecessors, it is only logical that the tempo of seat design and development has speeded up noticeably in America. The question of good lateral support was never particularly important when there was little or no lateral 'G' force, because of poor handling, but

189

competition experience has prompted more progress on this front.

This change has been more applicable in the United States than in Europe because we have always had twistier roads than America's great expanse of concrete highways. European cars have been better adapted to handling because of this, and even if Colorado has roads as twisty as the one alongside Loch Lomond, there are great areas of America that are uninterrupted by corners. In the past buyers have wanted big land cruisers with armchairs to give them the 'bordello look' and that boulevard ride, but that attitude is changing fast.

What is being asked for today is a high-performance seat with good support. The American market is even seeing this sort of development in the Ford Bronco and the Ranger truck, a 'two-by-four' two-wheel drive or four-wheel drive vehicle, fitted in some cases with bucket seats as standard equipment. So all these things have emerged which give a youthful, dynamic and progressive image for marketing purposes as well as being of practical benefit to the occupants.

Motor sport competition has given the world's largest manufacturing industry an opportunity to display its products in direct competition against rivals in the market place. True, some companies choose not to compete. Therefore, the ones who go out and do it have the courage, if you like, to say 'I'm up there being counted. If I don't win I'm still learning.'

The marketing that BMW, for example, has done from its touring car racing has been tremendous. Frankly, there are certain of their cars which I don't think handle particularly well, but the image they have surpasses any inherent restriction the car might have to perform the particular manoeuvres I might expect out of a particular model.

Sometimes, though, I am disappointed by the failure of some senior management in the motor industry to see the value of fully exercising the potential of their company's competition department. I'm constantly disappointed about the inclination to say 'that's the competition department. Shove them over at the other end of the factory. Even better still, get them out of the factory altogether. Keep them away from us. Racing or rallying has nothing to do with mainstream production.' That's wrong. What they should be saying is 'come inside, tell us what you have found, and if you've got something that's going to help us, why don't we have it now.' I don't think this attitude is adopted often enough. There is too much of a temptation to somehow regard competition departments as mavericks, rebels even. But the truth of the matter is that if they come up with anything new, you should look at it closely. These are not stodgy, run-of-the-mill engineers, they are creative innovators. They have to be, because if they're beaten this week they've got to change it for next week.

I firmly believe that there are many areas where competition development has still to contribute greatly towards road vehicle development, and the process is taking too long in some cases. How many cars have horizontally mounted rear dampers? Think of its application in respect of rear boot or trunk space in a saloon, an estate car or station wagon. It may appear to be unconventional and unuseable to some manufacturers, but the advantage in moving the shock absorbers from the vertical position to being laid down (as employed in racing cars over the years) is that the suspension can work just the same with adequate wheel movement, but without cluttering up the interior deck space of the vehicle. True, it may add $30 per car to do it today, and that's an abnormal amount of money in terms of production cost; perhaps this is the reason why it is not happening now. But I think it will.

Previously, the US market's experience with front-wheel drive had been limited, to say the least: the hulking Oldsmobile Toronado did not show off front-wheel drive qualities to best effect in the late Sixties!

When I'm testing for Ford and Goodyear, I am always trying to convince them that there is very much more to be learned out of motor sport testing procedures to benefit the street car or tyres, and that the best people to do ride and handling development and evaluation are young racing drivers. I would like to have a team of test drivers with single-seater experience because single-seaters are so adjustable. They have to learn about camber changes, roll bar stiffnesses, castor and cambers, toe-in and toe-out and so on, in practical terms. They learn that more completely and faster in a single-seater racing car because the cars are more sensitive to change. But, at the same time, they need to be able to come in and engineer their own changes and converse with the mechanics and engineers in their language.

I'm in my mid-forties and I think that I may want to do this for another five or six years. Maybe I'm wrong, and I'll go on doing it for another ten years, but the fact of the matter is I get so much pleasure and enjoyment out

The turbocharged Ford Mustang SV0 is a high performance machine which displays excellent ride and handling qualities, reflecting its competition parentage.

Changing tastes in external appearance: the aerodynamic Merkur XR4Ti was known in Europe as the Sierra XR4i, but its profile has become equally familiar on both sides of the Atlantic.

of this development work that I'm happy to continue with it for the moment. If I am going to leave any sort of legacy to Goodyear or Ford, it will be in the acceptance of the sort of test and development programmes which I have pursued over the years during my associations with these companies.

Perhaps some people are not quite convinced that my testing input is totally correct. Whether they will ever completely believe it, or whether I am in fact correct, is another question altogether. A good argument could be made to suggest that they know more about this type of testing than the people I would like to see take part. I would suggest that they may know more about engineering, but the truth is that some of the changes and fine tuning to a chassis are not as good as they could be. The feedback of an uncomfortable feeling that the engineering experts may miss, because they lack the inherent talent to carry out subjective analysis on the performance of a chassis, will ultimately affect the overall appreciation of a car by the purchaser.

You find a situation where the buyer perhaps does not feel totally comfortable in one particular type of car – but he does not know why. So he hops into another car that makes him feel comfortable, and that's the car he buys. We're talking about minute changes such as the valve setting in the operation of a power brake servo and the smoothness with which it comes in and out. An over-sensitive brake pedal action is another example of the sort of thing that can deter a potential buyer.

It may be that the engineer is satisfied through market research – which

Changing tastes in internal appearance: contrast the sumptuous yet confusing fasica of the 1965 Jaguar S-Type saloon with the 1985 Ford Granada Scorpio which offers increased information but in more straightforward fashion.

can be made to produce any result you like by the way in which the question is phrased – that Mr and Mrs Average want the reassurance which this instant brake response can provide. It might be said that sharpness will give them confidence. But, to somebody else, that sharpness may mean that they will never be able to sit in the back seat and read a newspaper!

The same applies to throttle application. Some engineers contend that if we have a progressive-rate throttle application, we should do it in reverse so that the early stage of the throttle application is the most rapid, to give an impression that the engine is more powerful than it actually is. I would say, on the other hand, that it would be preferable to have an engine which accelerates progressively and smoothly all the way up the performance range, with its most rapid response towards the end of the throttle pedal movement.

Most of the public don't know the engineering needs of a car. They seldom know what really is right. But if they were ever told what was right and how it would benefit them and make them feel more comfortable in their driving, if they knew how that over-sudden brake application factor could be to their disadvantage in the case of an incident by locking the brakes or even instigating an emergency which need not have been any more than a mild disturbance, then they would better appreciate the subtleties involved in making their car right.

You must attempt to give the public the absolute best. My point is that the evaluation of all the engineering talent and research input should be

The Ford RS200 rally prototype uses a similar four-wheel drive system to that employed in the Sierra XR 4x4 and Granada Scorpio saloons.

carried out by the most sensitive responders to mechanical movement or change – and that is a racing driver's profession. I don't see how you can expect an engineer to be a sufficiently outstanding driver to clearly evaluate the combination of sensations which is involved in assessing a vehicle's dymanics.

A racing driver's primary skill is being able to respond to movement of a car in action, which makes some of them (not all by any means) excellent test drivers. But they don't emerge from advertisements in the *Detroit News*, the *Akron Beacon Journal* or the *Birmingham Post*. It is wrong for any company to think that because a man is a good engineer and drives quite well that he is in a position to sense all that he has to in developing a multi-million dollar new product. A racing driver may not come up with a significantly different analysis on every occasion, but two or three times out of ten he is going to reveal something so significant that it really must be acknowledged. Oversights can be extremely expensive to rectify – ten or fifteen million dollars is nothing in this league!

This is why I am trying to get these small specialist groups together on both sides of the Atlantic. There is no question in my mind that there is untapped potential for many motor manufacturers to capitalise more on the talent they have available through motor sport for mainstream vehicle

development.

Above all, manufacturers need a stable of this talent which is not going to be affected by the transience of the company's promotional ladder. One of the best people I ever worked with in this connection at Ford was Dan Rivand, but all too soon promotion took him onward and upward into the Truck Division. I believe it would take between five and eight years to bring together three really good test drivers who could display the necessary awareness and communication skills that this specialist development role requires.

It worries me greatly that the sign-off procedures for products in many motor industry companies are left in the hands of individuals of questionable talent. Because a man has reached a certain level of importance in the management structure it does not mean he is a better driver. When he gets paid a large salary it will generally be for his abilities in a chosen field of endeavour, such as finance, sales, marketing, engineering or management of personnel. However, his increased status within the company will enable him to wield more influence and more corporate people will wish to please him, to bow to his opinions and wishes. This can be expensive.

In motor sport, this very seldom occurs. If Patrick Head is the designer in

*Audi's 4WD system was
introduced in the Quattro
coupé and gained
tremendous exposure
for its high-tech image
through rallying success.
The Quattro displayed
tremendous versatility in
rallying trim and won the
World Rally
Championship in 1982
and 1983.*

199

Formula 1, he does not test and evaluate his work. He tries to arrange that the best possible racing driver and development driver (hopefully one and the same man!) will be employed by the team. Only then will he be able to develop the full potential of his design concept. Head himself is not capable, as a driver, to interpret the car's various idiosyncrasies in a way which will allow it to be developed into a consistent winner. He will need one of the top half-dozen drivers in the world in order to realise that ambition and they will be very expensive. The chances of Head's car being developed to the maximum without the services of a top-line driver are extremely remote. Similarly, the chances of a top-line driver achieving success with a third-rate designer is equally unlikely. It's clear that you need the best possible talent in each particular area of importance.

My point is: get a specialist in each field of the highest level of competence that can possibly be afforded. I spent a great number of years developing my skills as a driver and got paid large sums of money for that talent. It is, therefore, fairly logical to assume that I know my business better than the man who only occasionally gets behind the wheel.

Likewise, the executives will more than likely be better than me in their particular spheres, as will the engineers. So let's recognise where our real skills lie. Let's not get carried away with what we *think* we can do. In motor sport we have to prove our talent in the cold light of competition against the best there is. Your worth is very clearly assessed by your successes and failures. If these lessons and principles are learned, I think there will be changes for the better in the motor industry as a whole – both from the car-maker's point of view and to the benefit of car buyers.

Chapter 6
The Road Application

Driving with finesse; that is the essence of being an efficient and sympathetic road driver. I always think that anyone who is driving a road vehicle should immediately become the epitome of the chauffeur, whatever the journey. His purpose is to instil an aura of confidence and comfort into all his passengers from the time that they close the door after getting into the car until they close the door at the end of the trip.

To accomplish these requirements you do not need engines revving and pulsating, waiting for the door to be closed or the seat belt finally to be clipped into place. There should be no whiplash effect of severe acceleration, affecting all the occupants from the baby to Grandma with equal ferocity, as the clutch is dropped suddenly and ferociously.

The same applies in the case of deceleration. There is no place for the screeching of brakes and tyres as you approach the traffic lights or intersection. The squealing of a tortured tyre as you go through a corner should only be indicative of inadequate inflation, not speed or the car's incorrect attitude to the corner. All of that is really bad driving.

If you make somebody feel nervous about the journey ahead, by over-exciting them with throttle application even when the car is still stationary, it gives them some premonition of what they are about to face. So why cause yourself trouble and create animosity for no reason? Similarly, if you are at a business meeting and make the man on the other side of the desk feel uncomfortable for any reason, the potential for success is much reduced.

When you start up an engine from cold and begin revving it hard immediately, the chances are you are going to do it more damage than anything else. The cylinder walls are not properly lubricated, the crankshaft is only half immersed in oil, the camshafts and top end of the engine are dry, the whole lubrication system hasn't got itself moving properly. So give your car a chance. If you don't you will pay for this lack of care at the end of the day, one way or another.

So learn just from the starting process: if you see any racing mechanic turning an engine over first thing in the morning, he'll turn it without even setting it alight. He'll turn it over without even switching the electrics on. We can't do that with a production road car engine, but, nevertheless, we should take note that if they are taking that much care, perhaps we should think more carefully about how we abuse our machine each day.

If we start up the engine without waking the neighbours with our high-revving cacophony that, in itself, is a nice gesture. Just let the engine tick over for a while, giving it an occasional, very gentle and ever-so mild throttle application. This will get you into the right mood because it doesn't feel nervous when you do that; it's a calm, almost lethargic movement. It's like the slow roll of a boat in the water, not a pitching feeling.

The same applies when you put the car into gear for the first time. Keep in mind that the clutch plate has to mesh against the flywheel and that gear has to be engaged smoothly. It doesn't have to baulk, to crunch. So when the engine revs a little bit and you depress the clutch, don't select the gear instantaneously. Give it a second or two for everything to find its way in gently and sympathetically. Feel it in gently, do it with finesse. That doesn't mean clenched fist and white knuckles, it means finger tips and thumb, usually. If it needs much more effort than that there's probably something wrong with it. You shouldn't have to over-exert yourself in this little task.

When you're letting the clutch out, do it in the same fluid manner. Feed it out gently and let the clutch take up, moving away in a nice, gentle application of power so that you don't actually feel the movement starting. There shouldn't be any flicking back of the head or pipes going through the newspaper. It should be completely progressive.

When you are changing gear with a cold engine, change up earlier than usual. The earlier you change gear, the less abrupt the effect of deceleration will be during that gearchange. So if there is an orange sector on the rev counter at 5000 rpm and a red sector at 5500 rpm, change up at just over 3000 rpm. It will be much pleasanter! The lower the gear, the earlier you should change. You might change from first to second at 2500 rpm, just enough for it to pull second. Grandma hasn't noticed because she's not particularly comfortable in the car in the first place: her wee legs are not quite reaching the floor properly, she's not really stable in the car and she's not looking the right way. So any movement backwards and forwards makes her uncomfortable.

The same applies going into third, fourth and fifth gears. Somehow, many people think that the better driver you are, the more gearchanges you need to make, both up and down, not to mention changing down as many times as possible when you are braking for a stop sign or a roundabout.

Not so! I'd rather use the brakes first because brake pads are cheaper to replace than gearboxes! Roll into a corner under braking, even in fourth gear, and put it directly into second gear when the time is right, but not when the car is going to nose down and the rear wheels lock momentarily while the revs shoot off the clock. There's no room for that.

So this whole image of 'boy, look at me, I'm an enthusiast driver' and the fact that I'm revving the engine mercilessly all the way through its performance range isn't actually doing anything for you. All it's doing is notifying the surrounding public of your impending arrival. They've heard you coming and they are just waiting for the accident or incident. And if, by some terrible misfortune, you do have an incident which is no fault of your own, to the dispassionate observer the very fact that you were driving in that manner puts you at fault in their mind. The accident may have had nothing at all to do with your driving, but the fashion in which you have been driving suggests that you were the one who was reckless.

Even though road driving is a long way apart from race driving and the one bears little relationship to the other, both require finesse and application of your personal sensitivity to the job in hand. When you are driving a competition car you are using all your intuition to get the maximum in terms of performance out of that car. While driving on the road you employ that effort to produce a docile ride for the benefit of your

When starting a car engine from cold, the thoughtful driver should be setting the tone for the whole journey. Allow the engine to warm up gently and progressively, with no violent revving or rough handling.

204

When you are selecting gears, the gearbox needs to warm up in exactly the same way as the engine, and should be coaxed rather than manhandled when the oil is still cold.

passengers, while treating other road users with consideration.

So don't rev the engine violently; change gear early and apply the brakes before down-shifting smoothly. The braking comes before the gearchanging on the way down, never the other way round. And the brake applications again should be smooth and progressive.

Consider a point which we have already examined in connection with the efficient performance of a competition car. Before you have even so much as touched the brakes, you must consider the way in which you come off the power. Don't come off the throttle pedal abruptly, but ease back on it gently. Just for once, drive down the road and come off the throttle abruptly and feel the jerk: then do it again, but ease off the throttle very progressively. In the latter case there is no jerk and you have not distracted your passengers from what they were saying or what they were reading. The same should apply when you press the brake. Do it gently and progressively and, before you have finished the braking motion, release the brake again very gently and progressively, so that you don't feel it coming off.

We have examined the manner in which such abrupt inputs can disturb

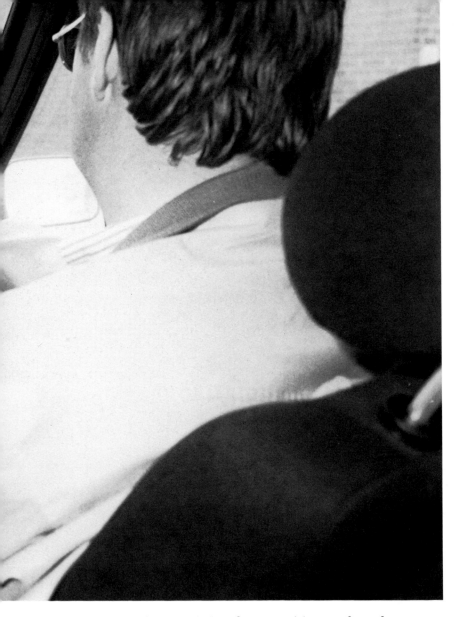

the ideal performance characteristics of a competition car, but when we are
considering the same aspects regarding a road car, we must remember that
a road car is more softly sprung and has greater suspension movement than
a racing car. It has more wheel movement, more roll, more dive and more
squat. All the movements are exaggerated compared with a competition
car.

That's why you benefit even more by driving smoothly in the manner I
have described. This is true also when you are changing direction. Don't
hang onto the steering wheel with white knuckles: it should be held with
fingers and thumbs and never, ever used as a grab handle. It was not
designed as a grab handle, it was designed to change the direction of the
vehicle. So sit in the seat in exactly the same way as I explained in the High
Speed Technique section. Be in a position to reach the steering wheel easily;
clench your fist round the top of the steering wheel and adjust your position
until the elbows are well bent. That will give you all the leverage you
require, particularly in an emergency when you might need to call on that
strength and leverage. Just remember, you don't see anybody lifting a

Wheelspin, opposite lock and frantic braking have no place at all in a road environment. Finesse should be the keynote of your driving technique; unruly behaviour will only attract adverse attention to your activities.

209

Try to keep away from any obstructions which might damage tyres or impose undue stress on suspension components. Kerbs are obvious hazards, but pot-holes, manhole covers and cats-eyes should also be avoided. Such care indicates a pride in one's driving technique.

heavy weight with a straight arm!

That is the first thing you do when you get into a car, although it is important that you can reach all the switches and see all the important instruments. This is as essential as if you were in the cockpit of a fighter plane – you should always be able to reach and see everything. You are probably going to have as many emergencies, one way or another, on the road as any racing driver may meet on the circuits.

Visibility over the steering wheel is also important. The belief that it is necessary to adopt a straight-arm driving style, like Farina or Stirling Moss appeared to use years ago, is a fallacy. Most racing drivers don't drive with straight arms at all, nor do they peer over the steering wheels. They need good visibility and have to be comfortable for long durations, whether to take part in long-distance events or simply to be able to put up with high G-forces.

Turning into a corner you must start off by moving the wheel a very small amount, then increase the lock progressively as you go through the corner. Think of it as a clock face. The first five minutes of the turn are slow and gentle, and then the next ten to fifteen minutes progressively get faster. And it's the same coming back. Taking off the lock through the first five minutes is relatively gentle, then it speeds up slightly and slows again in the last five minutes as you are completing the very last section of the corner.

Now, I wouldn't have espoused these theories fifteen or twenty years ago because I didn't know them then. I hadn't analysed my driving style to the same extent. That's why the reader must understand why I'm saying this and admitting that I didn't fully understand it twenty years ago. I might have known something about these matters, I might have exercised the technique in some way, but I certainly didn't fully understand all the elements involved.

In terms of pure mechanical driving technique, there is nothing I have done in a road car that isn't applicable in a race car and vice versa. The actual way in which you channel that technique is very different, fitting into a different set of priorities, but the bare bones of the technique are the same. I hope that my experiences will help young drivers to identify the various aspects of a car's behaviour, whether this is in a road or a track environment, and enable them to realise the direct connection between the two. If something is applicable to road driving technique, then, believe me, it is applicable to competition driving technique.

The next point to learn is how to read the road. We are not merely concerned with other road users now, but considering the uncluttered road with its manhole covers and water drainage grills. You should avoid driving close enough to the kerb to get the car bumping around badly. If you do, the car's ride is upset, you're putting more stress on the suspension, it's going to rattle more . . . so you don't drive that close to the kerb, ever. Similarly, if you see a manhole cover, avoid it. Don't wait until you get to one and then go round it like a pinball machine: look ahead and steer gently away from it.

Don't keep riding the reflective cats-eyes in the centre of the road. It's supremely irritating. If you're doing that you're not thinking. These are the little subtleties that your passengers will recognise and, subconsciously, will give you credit for. They may never notice it, but they may later be driven by somebody else and come back and say 'I don't know what you do that he doesn't, but I felt more comfortable with you'. The ultimate compliment to your driving ability is when they come to the end of their

Wrong on both counts! Bumping along the white line (top) is as bad as riding the kerb (bottom).

journey without realising how long they have been in the car.

Pay attention all the time. Watch out for bits of shredded tyres lying in the motorway. Don't run over them; make sure you notice them in time to change direction very slightly and unobtrusively, without any violent movement. The faster you are going, the smaller the degree of directional change you should be making, because, of course, if you make a major directional change at high speed you disturb the suspension more.

If you bear these points in mind, the chances are that your shock absorbers will last longer, the car will develop fewer rattles, the transmission will last longer, your fuel consumption will be reduced, your tyre mileage will be increased and you will be a less fatigued driver.

Although it may sound awfully old-fashioned, slightly pompous and

Changing lanes on motorways should be carried out in one smooth, unobtrusive and almost imperceptible movement. Sudden swerving can upset the car and create a potentially dangerous situation.

'do-gooding', the three 'Cs' are quite useful when bearing in mind how to drive. Firstly, you have to *concentrate*; you have to be a *conscientious* driver more than anything else, because if you are a conscientious driver you will concentrate as a matter of course; thirdly, you have to be *considerate*.

If you are considerate to other road users, you are reading the road, reading the traffic patterns. You notice the driver who is trying to get out of the side road: sooner or later he's going to cause a problem. He's having his blood pressure upped pretty dramatically, and in the end he is probably going to drive out in front of somebody else and cause their blood pressure to shoot up pretty wildly, too!

So wait a minute, give him priority if you can, it's no big deal. OK, so you may be in a hurry, but if you are, signal to him, 'scrry, look I'm in a

Consideration should also be a factor when driving on the road; if you can, offer right of way to fellow road users.

hurry . . .' Communicate, be considerate. Now that may sound rather fuddy-duddy, but in terms of the three 'Cs' it's a good attitude to have.

Let's think about applying these qualities of consideration and anticipation to the overtaking manoeuvre, for example. We should never slipstream a sixteen-wheel articulated truck when we are on the motorway, slingshooting our way past. It can surprise a truck driver to see this flash of metal coming out from beneath his rear wheels, as well as to the driver who is minding his own business in the fast lane and is suddenly faced with your erratic, abrupt change of direction.

Gentle, progressive overtaking, and gentle, progressive rejoining of whatever lane you find correct for you is such a nice way to drive. You can drive without really feeling any significant sense of motion from a car if you do it correctly. That allows you to be consciously a very conscientious driver because you can do it commuting to the office, on a pleasure trip or on an afternoon drive. The need to make it a smooth journey means that you've got to sit and *drive* the car for the entire trip. Each gearchange is a challenge, each stop, even in a traffic jam, is an opportunity.

That is the positive aspect of actually enjoying your driving and making yourself enjoy it by giving yourself that challenge. It leads to pride and satisfaction in what you are doing.

It seems to have been a long time since I toured Europe with the Formula Finesse competition, the 'ball in the dish' exercise which we later took on a country-wide tour in Britain and, more recently, introduced to the USA.

That theory and concept still works effectively and accurately today as an index of how well a driver is displaying his technique. If you drive very smoothly and progressively, on acceleration, braking and cornering, the ball stays in the salad bowl. But the moment you steer round the corner like a fifty pence piece, having several bites at the corner, the ball will come out of the bowl.

That was one practical way of demonstrating to people that some of them drove differently from me. Of course, they say there are only two ways of truly insulting a man – tell him he's a bad lover, or he's a bad driver! He will never be convinced about either argument.

Now I cannot demonstrate the loving too easily, but I can demonstrate the driving, using the Formula Finesse technique. It has been a very useful exercise for me, in effect, to say to you, the reader, 'Hey, you're not driving too well'. You may reply, 'Don't be ridiculous'. So we go and do a little Formula Finesse exercise. You may think you do it correctly, but not today. Look, there's the ball bouncing out of the bowl. There's the proof.

I think it is appropriate to draw the importance of developing such a technique to the attention of the many young drivers who will be reading this book. On a personal note, I certainly recall being involved in innumerable incidents at the wheel in my youth, between the ages of 17 and 20 years. Little incidents and minor comings together . . . this was not on a race track, remember. I think it is clear from the statistics, however disappointing it might seem, that young drivers are the most at risk – much as I admire youth and, indeed, yearn for it sometimes! That exuberance behind the wheel is something you have to experience and, hopefully, learn from. Categorically, speed is for the race track, *not* for the road.

Let's turn now to the differing techniques involved with different transmission configurations. As I write this book, I tend to think when we look back on the history of motoring in the years to come, there will be a front-wheel drive period. There was an era when front-wheel drive was thought to be the be-all and end-all of technical configurations.

Front-wheel drive will probably continue to exist with small-engined cars, but I think that four-wheel drive will become much more prevalent in the future. It makes a lot more sense.

Historically, the balance of the car as the driver has known it is with rear-wheel drive, and that's where the best 'feel' has come from. There are a few isolated areas where front-wheel drive has been of considerable benefit, such as rallying, some off-road activities and particularly in snow, but in those situations the drivers created the rear-wheel drive feel by left-foot braking, getting the back to swing out and allowing the car to pull itself out of the corners while pointing in the right direction. But, as we know today, the best balance comes from a rear-wheel drive machine.

I have never been a great supporter of front-wheel drive and some of the past American efforts with this configuration in large cars – such as the Oldsmobile Toronado – were not successful. Their incredibly large cast-iron block engines, mated to huge transmission systems, seemed to me like the ultimate mechanical nightmare, with all the potential for oil leaks and corrosions, rubber doughnuts, joints and gaiters all weeping and perishing, plus lots of vibrations, clunks and clanks. On the other hand, Alex Issigonis's Mini was one of the greatest contributions to the history of the car. As a small car concept it was excellent.

The Audi Quattro was a great step forward and hailed as the best-handling high-performance car, with its four-wheel drive system. Yet, on a test track, I found that it had quite distinct limitations – shortcomings in fact. And that also applies on the road in extreme circumstances. I don't think it was all that remarkable as a handling package.

In my view, whatever four-wheel drive did for it, its 'brains' were still over the front wheel. It was a front-wheel drive car which was converted to be a four-wheel drive car. Its personality never really changed: all the messages still came from the front end, finding their way to the rear wheels almost as a second thought.

However, I think that the FF Developments system, recently adopted by Ford for the Sierra XR4 and the Granada Scorpio (both of which started out as rear-wheel drive cars and evolved into four-wheel drive cars) is better. The Ford RS200 rally car feels better on dry tarmac in four-wheel drive than it does with rear-wheel drive.

Although, on the face of it, many people consider it to be quite logical for a car to be driven through all four of its wheels, the transmission systems still represent such a cost penalty as to prevent them being incorporated in volume production cars as a matter of course at the time of writing.

Regarding competition cars, I had experience of the early BRM 4WD, the Matra MS84 and the Cosworth. I was supposed to drive one of the Lotus turbine cars at Indianapolis in 1968, but that never happened.

To sum up, though, I like four-wheel drive because of its added sense of security and the practical advantages. It makes me feel that little bit more sure that I'm going to get to the top of the hill in winter. I like the fact it is there for my wife and family. It instils more confidence and obviously indicates the way in which road cars will develop in the future. Keep in mind that a large part of the USA, for example, lives in potential snow conditions for almost one-third of each year. That includes the eastern seaboard north of Washington, much of the mid-west, the north-west and Colorado, while a large part of Europe would also benefit from four-wheel drive for safety reasons for much of the year.

Just as wet-weather driving on the track calls for a delicacy of touch, the same factors apply to driving in the rain on the road. Although road engines are far more docile propositions compared with their racing contemporaries, and modern road tyres provide an impressive level of grip under acceleration and braking, the same basic restrictions apply.

However you consider it, you have less grip than in the dry. And remember that many roads frequently have changes of surface which can catch you out in wet conditions, some giving slightly more adhesion, some slightly less. You should watch for puddles or a build-up of standing water in the gutters. The painted road markings can be especially slippery. You must think ahead clearly and anticipate changes in conditions. Remember, it is important to leave an additional margin to accommodate sudden and unexpected manoeuvres on the part of other road users. If somebody brakes abruptly and pulls across in front of you, react smoothly and confidently; there should be no sudden movements.

The application of the 'Formula Finesse' approach takes on an even more important emphasis in the wet. The problems caused by sudden steering input, harsh acceleration in the lower gears and over-energetic braking will be aggravated, increasing the possibility of a slide or a skid. The trend towards anti-lock brakes is a commendable development amongst the world's car manufacturers, but it is merely an adjunct to smooth and sensible driving. However good the equipment, it is the operator that matters, and in this case the operator is the driver.

Finally, remember that one of the most important, if too easily forgotten, precepts for driving under any conditions is adequate preparation. In poor weather conditions this means making sure that your car is ready to deal with rain, snow, sleet or slush. Make certain that the headlights are clean before you set out on your journey. Ensure that the windscreen washer reservoirs are full, the wiper blades are in good condition. Warm up the car for a few moments to ensure that the demisting system is working. It will only cost you a small amount of time but it may give you a split-second advantage in which to extract yourself from a potentially hazardous situation during your journey.

We have a love affair with the motor car – and for many of those who read this book it is a deeply satisfying and lasting relationship. Cars can be like wonderful friends, providing us with enormous pleasure as well as convenience, but the way in which we apply ourselves to their use can make the difference between their being friend or foe. The car can become extremely dangerous in the wrong hands – or even in the right hands, but the wrong mood. We cannot all be a talented pilot, skilled neurosurgeon or World Champion. But almost everyone can improve on their present level of competence, and our attitudes have probably greater influence on our levels of success than do any basic skills.

Chapter 7
On a Personal Note

Motor sport, for me, will never be replaced from the point of view of the excitement, exhilaration and personal satisfaction I derived from it. The feeling of achievement and the sheer unadulterated pleasure I experienced from driving a car at the limit of its ability, and my own, will live with me for ever.

It is a very selfish sport, a self-satisfying endeavour and, having said that, I don't apologise for having selfishly taken pleasure from the sport while at the same time recognising I was well rewarded in a material sense. But the rewards I got out of motor racing were far deeper than in just a monetary sense. There is nothing that I would change if I had my time over again apart, obviously, from some of the tyre marks on the road which marked accidents in which drivers, friends, were lost in the sport.

Yet even that element of it was an essential aspect of the overall picture, I suppose. There is nothing in life that has any real value to you unless it costs you in some way. If you buy something wonderfully luxurious, the chances are it costs you a great deal of money. If something gives you intense pleasure, something has to be given in exchange. Some day, a repayment becomes due. Life has a way of calling in its debts, and motor racing, for all the satisfaction and pleasure I derived from it, perhaps exacted its price in terms of the accidents which happened to others.

Those accidents made me extremely sad, but perhaps that is what made the sport such a strong light in my life. Those tragedies opened up great caverns of depression, but somehow those caverns and dark corners were illuminated by this rose-coloured light which seemed to dominate my whole being when I climbed into the cockpit of a Grand Prix car.

Nothing in my life will ever replace that – in fact, I would not even attempt to find any other activity to replace it. It's just part of my past, and I suppose I am one of the rare exceptions to the rule who has left the sport with no regrets whatsoever as an active participant.

I often liken it to eating Mars bars, or Snickers in America: I love them, and if you gave me a whole box of them I would systematically devour them all. If I think of my motor racing as a box of chocolate bars, every one was a great flavour and great taste. But I chose to finish, so to speak, before I had eaten the last bar. Had I eaten the last bar, I think I might have been sick and might never have wanted to eat another one in my life. But my stomach was full from eating the penultimate bar and I never touched the last one in the box; I walked away from the sport with no regrets at all, still retaining a great love for it.

What's more, I have never had the desire to return. Not once since I

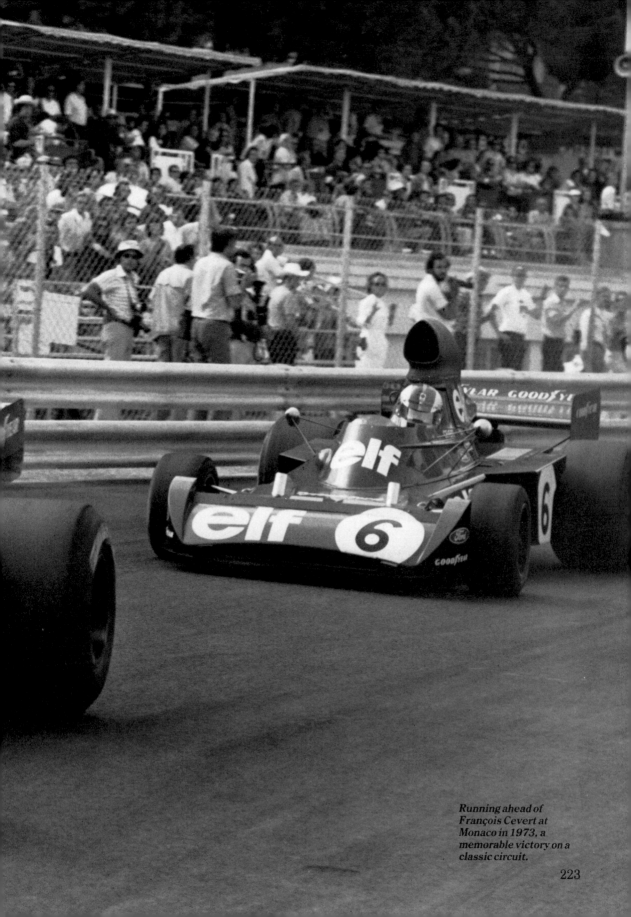

Running ahead of
François Cevert at
Monaco in 1973, a
memorable victory on a
classic circuit.

Monza 1969, when I clinched my first World Championship. Here my Matra leads the pack into Parabolica.

stopped driving have I had the slightest inclination to return as an active driver, and for that I'm very grateful indeed. But I'm even more grateful for the fact that I don't detest the sport. I never got sick of it, I didn't leave it with a bitter taste in my mouth.

I'm not now one of those people who profess not to understand why those people competing today actually take part in the sport; you won't find me suggesting that they are mad for doing so. I take my hat off to them: I *know* why they do it, and I hope they enjoy it as much as I did. I cherish the pleasure I derived from my participation very dearly indeed.

Also, I am fortunate that I am still allowed the privilege of driving whenever I like. The work that I do with Ford and Goodyear today means that, on some occasions I am in a car five days a week on a test track, driving

those cars to the limit of their potential. They may not be the most powerful racing machines in the world, but they are still being tested to their limits and my own. This means I am still exercising my original talents to the full and I'm delighted to live with that.

All this provides a very important element in my continuing affection for the sport. The material benefits afforded me and my family are tremendous. The homes we have, the manner in which we live, the friends we enjoy, the *entrées* which have been made available to me – all of those things are the product of motor racing. Without motor racing Jackie Stewart would not be the individual he is today, he would not be able to do the many things he does that are no longer directly associated with motor sport.

So, from every angle I can think of, my life has been lit by that strong rose-coloured light that has obliterated almost every shadow. That is something that any man should be grateful for.

As far as my campaigning on matters of safety was concerned, all I can say is that I'm glad I tackled it so aggressively. I may have ruffled a few establishment feathers along the way, but I think it had to be done. Those feathers needed ruffling and, indeed, some of them had to be plucked out. There may, so to speak, be some bald birds running around blaming me for their lack of plumage!

Perhaps I could have stayed closely involved with racing for longer immediately after I retired from the cockpit. But the sport is an animal

Postscript: testing road cars for Goodyear and Ford allows me to put into practice the lessons and techniques learned during my racing years. This work is a source of enduring pleasure to me.

which feels dependent on personal involvements: I was never asked by the governing body to take an active part in that particular area and, at the time, I wasn't ready to do so in any case. My life was very full, occupied with other commitments.

On the commercial side I'm glad I saw the opportunities I did and pleased that some of the things I did rubbed off and, of course, the sport has become a commercial giant since I retired. But I feel I have been part of that movement, all of which has been very positive and beneficial for the sport as a whole. My regret is that most of the drivers have not appreciated with the same foresight the benefits that can be realised and have allowed themselves, somehow or other, almost to be overshadowed by the sport rather than remaining in the spotlight, centre stage.

The Constructors' Association was created almost in the fear that the drivers would continue to have the prominence and power that I was enjoying when I was at the pinnacle of my career. I think this was very threatening to a lot of people in the business who felt this situation should never be permitted to develop again. But the drivers have allowed themselves to be suffocated far too much and they do not have the power and position in the sport today that they should have.

It was my experience when I was President of the Grand Prix Drivers' Association that the drivers themselves are sadly lethargic about even those matters which would be to their benefit, and even more lethargic towards anything benefiting fellow competitors. They have somehow allowed themselves to become bypassed, used and sometimes abused in a fashion which I find very distasteful. But, on the other hand, if people are prepared to be walked on, then they will be used as carpets. It is their own doing. No-one seems to be prepared to stand up and put in the work necessary to earn that position of authority and power.

After all, at the end of the day, however big may be the names of Ferrari, Lotus, Brabham, Williams and Tyrrell, it is the drivers who sit in those cars and conduct them – the human element and the focal point of the public interest. And yet those people do not seem to have the prominence that they deserve. That I regret, but I don't blame myself at all. I'm sad that others have not seen this point as active competitors.

Apart from that, I cannot think of any area where I feel my personal fulfilment has failed to be fully realised.

Monza in 1969 was a big moment: winning the race and the Championship, although I was never totally confident that my decision to use a special long fourth gear which I could hold all the way to the finishing line on the last lap would actually work. I had the correct equipment; I was just uncertain whether I could utilise it to the best effect – whether I would be correctly placed on the track or, indeed, would miss a gear.

I cannot recall one isolated moment of satisfaction which stands out from my whole career, but I can think back and remember how satisfying it was over an entire weekend at Monaco to have been fastest in every session, then lead all the way and win the race. To be able just to go out, switch on and do it was very satisfying indeed. Oddly enough, there were no joyous moments as such, in the purest sense. And this was for a very good reason. I always worked so hard to suppress and eliminate emotions from my whole presence when I was competing, that the feeling of buoyant satisfaction was never allowed to manifest itself. Really, my mind was so heavily programmed to eliminate both anger or elation that I robbed myself of a lot of very happy times, a lot of spontaneous pleasure.

I have a photograph of the winner's rostrum at Paul Ricard after I won

227

the French Grand Prix in 1971, where François Cevert was second. There is a massive crowd all round us: François is jubilant! But I'm standing up there, the winner, just looking at this china trophy, holding it up and looking at the signature to make sure it's an original piece. Here is this massive crowd cheering the top finishers: one is young, bright-eyed and delighted to be second. The winner is the old man trying to price the trophy . . . that, to me, always brings back the reality of how I was in those days.

Jackie Stewart: Chronology

1939

Born 11 June, Dumbarton, Scotland

1959/60

Won British, Scottish, Irish, Welsh and English trap shooting championships. Failed narrowly to be selected for British Olympic team in 1960.

1962

First race at Charterhall, Scotland, in Marcos sports car owned by Barry Filer.

1963

Drove for Ecurie Ecosse in Cooper-Monaco sports car.

Leading F3 Cooper-BMC team-mate Warwick Banks, Silverstone, 1964.

1964

14 March	Snetterton	F3 Cooper-BMC	1st
21 March	Oulton Park	Tojeiro-Buick GT	Retired
		Cooper-Monaco	1st
		Lotus Cortina	1st
30 March	Goodwood	F3 Cooper-BMC	1st
		Cooper Monaco	2nd
11 April	Oulton Park	F3 Cooper-BMC	1st in class
		Lotus Cortina	5th
		Cooper-Monaco	Practice crash
18 April	Aintree	F3 Cooper-BMC	1st
		Lotus Cortina	6th
2 May	Silverstone	F3 Cooper-BMC	1st
		Tojeiro-Ford GT	6th
		Lotus Elan	3rd
9 May	Monaco	F3 Cooper-BMC	1st
17 May	Mallory Park	F3 Cooper-BMC	1st
		Lotus Elan	1st
18 May	Goodwood	Tojeiro-Ford GT	Retired
24 May	Montlhéry	Lotus-Ford prototype	4th
7 June	La Chartre	F3 Cooper-BMC	2nd
13 June	Crystal Palace	Jaguar E-type	1st
		Lotus Elan	1st
		Jaguar XK120	1st
28 June	Rouen	F3 Cooper-BMC	1st
5 July	Reims (12-hours)	Ferrari GTO	17th (sharing with Chris Amon)
11 July	Brands Hatch	Jaguar E-type	2nd
		Lotus Cortina	3rd
		Tojeiro-Ford GT	8th
19 July	Clermont-Ferrand	F2 Lotus-Ford	2nd
3 August	Brands Hatch	Jaguar E-type	Retired
		Lotus Elan	1st
		F3 Cooper-BMC	6th
9 August	Karlskoga	F3 Cooper-BMC	Non-starter
23 August	Zolder	F2 Lotus-Ford	Retired
		F3 Cooper-BMC	Retired
30 August	Zandvoort	F3 Cooper-BMC	1st
13 September	Albi	F2 Lotus-Ford	Retired
19 September	Oulton Park	F2 Lotus-Ford	3rd
		F3 Cooper-BMC	1st
26 September	Snetterton	F3 Cooper-BMC	1st
27 September	Montlhéry	F2 Lotus-Ford	2nd
4 October	Montlhéry	Lotus Cortina	1st
11 October	Montlhéry	Ferrari 250LM	10th (with Ludovico Scarfiotti)
29 November	Sandown Park	Lotus Cortina	Retired (sharing with Jim Palmer)
12 December	Kyalami	Lotus 33 F1	Unplaced; winner in 2nd of two heats

1965

1 January	South African GP, East London	BRM V8	6th
13 March	Race of Champions, Brands Hatch	BRM V8	2nd
3 April	Oulton Park	F2 Cooper-BRM	2nd
10 April	Snetterton	F2 Cooper-BRM	Retired
19 April	Goodwood	BRM V8	Retired
25 April	Pau	F2 Cooper-BRM	5th
15 May	International Trophy, Silverstone	BRM V8	1st
23 May	1000 kms Nürburgring	Ferrari P2	Retired (sharing Graham Hill)
30 May	MONACO GP	BRM V8	3rd
7 June	Crystal Palace	F2 Cooper-BRM	Retired
13 June	BELGIAN GP	BRM V8	2nd
19/20 June	Le Mans	Rover BRM turbine	10th (sharing with Graham Hill)
27 June	FRENCH GP	BRM V8	2nd
4 July	Reims	F2 Cooper-BRM	5th
10 July	BRITISH GP	BRM V8	5th
11 July	Rouen	F2 Cooper-BRM	Retired
17 July	DUTCH GP	BRM V8	2nd
1 August	GERMAN GP	BRM V8	Retired
8 August	Karlskoga	F2 Cooper-BRM	Retired
30 August	Brands Hatch	Lola T70	3rd
12 September	ITALIAN GP	BRM V8	1st
18 September	Gold Cup, Oulton Park	F2 Cooper-BRM	Retired
3 October	US GP	BRM V8	Retired
24 October	MEXICAN GP	BRM V8	Retired

Finishing second in 1965 Belgian GP for BRM.

1966

8 January	New Zealand GP	BRM V8	2nd
15 January	Levin	BRM V8	Retired
22 January	Lady Wigram Trophy	BRM V8	1st
29 January	Teretonga	BRM V8	1st
13 February	Warwick Farm	BRM V8	4th
20 February	Australian GP	BRM V8	Retired
27 February	Sandown Park	BRM V8	1st
7 March	Longford, Tasmania	BRM V8	1st
26 March	Sebring 12-hours	Ford GT40	Retired (sharing with Graham Hill)
11 April	Goodwood	F2 Matra-BRM	6th
17 April	Pau	F2 Matra-BRM	4th
24 April	Barcelona	F2 Matra-Ford	2nd
22 May	MONACO GP	BRM V8	1st
30 May	Indianapolis 500	Lola-Ford	Retired
4 June	Mosport Park	Lola T70	Retired
12 June	BELGIAN GP	BRM V8	Crashed
16 July	BRITISH GP	BRM V8	Retired
24 July	DUTCH GP	BRM V8	4th
31 July	Snetterton	Lotus Cortina	4th
7 August	GERMAN GP	BRM V8	5th
14 August	Surfers Paradise	Brabham-Repco	Retired
21 August	Surfers Paradise	Ferrari 250LM	2nd (sharing with Andrew Buchanan)
4 September	ITALIAN GP	BRM H16	Retired
11 September	Montlhéry	F2 Matra-Ford	4th
17 September	Gold Cup, Oulton Park	BRM H16	Retired
18 September	Le Mans Bugatti	F2 Matra-Ford	4th
25 September	Albi	F2 Matra-Ford	Retired
2 October	US GP	BRM H16	Retired
9 October	Fuji	Lola-Ford	1st
23 October	MEXICAN GP	BRM H16	Retired
30 October	Riverside	Lola T70	Retired
13 November	Las Vegas	Lola T70	Retired

1967

2 January	SOUTH AFRICAN GP	BRM H16	Retired
7 January	New Zealand GP	BRM V8	1st
14 January	Levin	BRM V8	2nd
21 January	Lady Wigram Trophy	BRM V8	Retired
12 February	Lakeside	BRM V8	Retired
19 February	Australian GP	BRM V8	1st
26 February	Sandown Park	BRM V8	Retired
6 March	Longford, Tasmania	BRM V8	Retired
24 March	Snetterton	F2 Matra-Ford	Retired
27 March	Silverstone	F2 Matra-Ford	5th
2 April	Pau	F2 Matra-Ford	Retired
9 April	Barcelona	F2 Matra-Ford	Retired
15 April	Oulton Park	BRM H16	Retired
29 April	International Trophy, Silverstone	BRM H16	Retired
7 May	MONACO GP	BRM V8	Retired
30 May	Indianapolis 500	Lola-Ford	Retired
4 June	DUTCH GP	BRM H16	Retired
18 June	BELGIAN GP	BRM H16	2nd
25 June	Reims	F2 Matra-Ford	4th
2 July	FRENCH GP	BRM V8	3rd
9 July	Rouen	F2 Matra-Ford	Retired
15 July	BRITISH GP	BRM H16	Retired
23 July	Jarama	F2 Matra-Ford	2nd
30 July	BOAC 1000 kms, Brands Hatch	Ferrari 330P4	2nd (sharing with Chris Amon)
6 August	GERMAN GP	BRM H16	Retired
13 August	Karlskoga	F2 Matra-Ford	1st
20 August	Enna	F2 Matra-Ford	1st
27 August	CANADIAN GP	BRM H16	Retired
28 August	Brands Hatch	F2 Matra-Ford	2nd
10 September	ITALIAN GP	BRM H16	Retired
16 September	Gold Cup, Oulton Park	F2 Matra-Ford	2nd
24 September	Albi	F2 Matra-Ford	1st
1 October	US GP	BRM H16	Retired
22 October	MEXICAN GP	BRM H16	Retired
12 November	Jarama	F2 Matra-Ford	Retired

Leading Indy 500 for Lola, 1966.

1968

Date	Event	Car	Result
1 January	SOUTH AFRICAN GP	F1 Matra-Ford	Retired
17 March	Race of Champions, Brands Hatch	F1 Matra-Ford	6th
31 March	Barcelona	F2 Matra-Ford	1st
24 April	Pau	F2 Matra-Ford	1st
28 April	Jarama	F2 Matra-Ford	Practice crash
9 June	BELGIAN GP	F1 Matra-Ford	4th
23 June	DUTCH GP	F1 Matra-Ford	1st
7 July	FRENCH GP	F1 Matra-Ford	3rd
20 July	BRITISH GP	F1 Matra-Ford	6th
4 August	GERMAN GP	F1 Matra-Ford	1st
17 August	Gold Cup, Oulton Park	F1 Matra-Ford	1st
8 September	ITALIAN GP	F1 Matra-Ford	Retired
15 September	Reims	F2 Matra-Ford	1st
22 September	CANADIAN GP	F1 Matra-Ford	6th
6 October	US GP	F1 Matra-Ford	1st
20 October	Albi	F2 Matra-Ford	Retired
3 November	MEXICAN GP	F1 Matra-Ford	7th

1969

1 March	SOUTH AFRICAN GP	F1 Matra-Ford	1st
16 March	Race of Champions, Brands Hatch	F1 Matra-Ford	1st
30 March	International Trophy, Silverstone	F1 Matra-Ford	3rd
7 April	Thruxton	F2 Matra-Ford	2nd
20 April	Pau	F2 Matra-Ford	Retired
27 April	Nürburgring	F2 Matra-Ford	1st
4 May	SPANISH GP	F1 Matra-Ford	1st
11 May	Jarama	F2 Matra-Ford	1st
18 May	MONACO GP	F1 Matra-Ford	Retired
8 June	Zolder	F2 Matra-Ford	Retired
21 June	DUTCH GP	F1 Matra-Ford	1st
29 June	Reims	F2 Matra-Ford	4th
6 July	FRENCH GP	F1 Matra-Ford	1st
13 July	Tulln-Langenlebarn	F2 Matra-Ford	2nd
19 July	BRITISH GP	F1 Matra-Ford	1st
3 August	GERMAN GP	F1 Matra-Ford	2nd
16 August	Gold Cup, Oulton Park	F1 Matra-Ford	Retired
9 September	ITALIAN GP	F1 Matra-Ford	1st
14 September	Albi	F2 Matra-Ford	Retired
20 September	CANADIAN GP	F1 Matra-Ford	Retired
5 October	US GP	F1 Matra-Ford	Retired
19 October	MEXICAN GP	F1 Matra-Ford	4th

On the way to victory in 1968 Dutch GP in Matra MS80.

1970

7 March	SOUTH AFRICAN GP	F1 Matra-Ford	3rd
22 March	Race of Champions, Brands Hatch	F1 March 701	1st
30 March	Thruxton	F2 Brabham-Ford	2nd
19 April	SPANISH GP	F1 March-Ford	1st
26 April	International Trophy,	F1 March-Ford	2nd
3 May	Japanese GP	F2 Brabham-Ford	1st
10 May	MONACO GP	F1 March-Ford	Retired
24 May	Brands Hatch	Ford Capri	5th
25 May	Crystal Palace	F2 Brabham-Ford	1st
7 June	BELGIAN GP	F1 March-Ford	Retired
21 June	DUTCH GP	F1 March-Ford	2nd
27 June	Tourist Trophy	Ford Escort	Retired
5 July	FRENCH GP	F1 March-Ford	8th
12 July	Watkins Glen	Chaparral-Chevy	Retired
18 July	BRITISH GP	F1 March-Ford	Retired
26 July	Paul Ricard	F2 Brabham-Ford	Retired
2 August	GERMAN GP	F1 March-Ford	Retired
16 August	AUSTRIAN GP	F1 March-Ford	Retired
22 August	Gold Cup, Oulton Park	F1 Tyrrell-Ford	Retired
6 September	ITALIAN GP	F1 March-Ford	2nd
20 September	CANADIAN GP	F1 Tyrrell-Ford	Retired
4 October	US GP	F1 Tyrrell-Ford	Retired
25 October	MEXICAN GP	F1 Tyrrell-Ford	Retired

Victory run at Nürburgring, 1971, Tyrrell-Ford.

1971

Date	Event	Car	Result
6 March	SOUTH AFRICAN GP	F1 Tyrrell-Ford	2nd
21 March	Race of Champions, Brands Hatch	F1 Tyrrell-Ford	2nd
28 March	Ontario, Calif.	F1 Tyrrell-Ford	2nd
10 April	Oulton Park	F1 Tyrrell-Ford	3rd
18 April	SPANISH GP	F1 Tyrrell-Ford	1st
5 May	International Trophy, Silverstone	F1 Tyrrell-Ford	Retired
23 May	MONACO GP	F1 Tyrrell-Ford	1st
13 June	Mosport Park	Can-Am Lola	Retired
20 June	Dutch GP	F1 Tyrrell-Ford	11th
27 June	Mont Tremblant	Can-Am Lola	1st
4 July	FRENCH GP	F1 Tyrrell-Ford	1st
11 July	Road Atlanta	Can-Am Lola	Retired
17 July	BRITISH GP	F1 Tyrrell-Ford	1st
25 July	Watkins Glen	Can-Am Lola	Retired
1 August	GERMAN GP	F1 Tyrrell-Ford	1st
15 August	AUSTRIAN GP	F1 Tyrrell-Ford	Retired
22 August	Mid Ohio	Can-Am Lola	1st
29 August	Elkhart Lake	Can-Am Lola	Retired
5 September	ITALIAN GP	F1 Tyrrell-Ford	Retired
12 September	Donnybrooke	Can-Am Lola	6th
19 September	CANADIAN GP	F1 Tyrrell-Ford	1st
26 September	Edmonton	Can-Am Lola	2nd
3 October	US GP	F1 Tyrrell-Ford	5th
17 October	Laguna Seca	Can-Am Lola	2nd
24 October	F1 Brands Hatch	F1 Tyrrell-Ford	3rd
31 October	Riverside	Can-Am Lola	

1972

23 January	ARGENTINE GP	F1 Tyrrell-Ford	1st
4 March	SOUTH AFRICAN GP	F1 Tyrrell-Ford	Retired
1 May	SPANISH GP	F1 Tyrrell-Ford	Retired
14 May	MONACO GP	F1 Tyrrell-Ford	4th
2 July	FRENCH GP	F1 Tyrrell-Ford	1st
15 July	BRITISH GP	F1 Tyrrell-Ford	2nd
30 July	GERMAN GP	F1 Tyrrell-Ford	Retired
13 August	AUSTRIAN GP	F1 Tyrrell-Ford	7th
3 September	Paul Ricard	Ford Capri	2nd (with François Cevert)
10 September	ITALIAN GP	F1 Tyrrell-Ford	Retired
24 September	CANADIAN GP	F1 Tyrrell-Ford	1st
8 October	US GP	F1 Tyrrell-Ford	1st

Opening 1972 with a win in Argentina.

1973

28 January	ARGENTINE GP	F1 Tyrrell-Ford	3rd
11 February	BRAZILIAN GP	F1 Tyrrell-Ford	2nd
3 March	SOUTH AFRICAN GP	F1 Tyrrell-Ford	1st
25 March	Monza	Ford Capri	Retired
8 April	International Trophy, Silverstone	F1 Tyrrell-Ford	1st
29 April	SPANISH GP	F1 Tyrrell-Ford	Retired
20 May	BELGIAN GP	F1 Tyrrell-Ford	1st
3 June	MONACO GP	F1 Tyrrell-Ford	1st
17 June	SWEDISH GP	F1 Tyrrell-Ford	5th
1 July	FRENCH GP	F1 Tyrrell-Ford	4th
8 July	Nürburgring	Ford Capri	Retired
14 July	BRITISH GP	F1 Tyrrell-Ford	10th
29 July	DUTCH GP	F1 Tyrrell-Ford	1st
5 August	GERMAN GP	F1 Tyrrell-Ford	1st
19 August	AUSTRIAN GP	F1 Tyrrell-Ford	2nd
2 September	Paul Ricard	Ford Capri	5th (with Jochen Mass)
9 September	ITALIAN GP	F1 Tyrrell-Ford	4th
23 September	CANADIAN GP	F1 Tyrrell-Ford	5th

Career at a glance: 99 Grand Prix starts, 27 victories. 17 pole positions; 42 front row starts. 11 second places, 5 third places, 6 fourth places, 5 fifth places, 3 sixth places. World Champion 1969, 1971 and 1973. 15 fastest race laps.

Last win: German GP, Nürburgring, 1973.